KNIT
with
LOVE

KNIT

with

LOVE

STORIES TO WARM
A KNITTER'S HEART

Lisa Bogart

Revell

a division of Baker Publishing Group
Grand Rapids, Michigan

© 2011 by Lisa Bogart

Published by Revell
a division of Baker Publishing Group
P.O. Box 6287, Grand Rapids, MI 49516-6287
www.revellbooks.com

Printed in the United States of America

Library of Congress Cataloging-in-Publication Data
Bogart, Lisa, 1960–
    Knit with love : stories to warm a knitter's heart / Lisa Bogart.
       p.   cm.
    Includes bibliographical references.
    ISBN 978-0-8007-1970-8 (pbk.)
      1. Knitters (Persons)—Prayers and devotions. 2. Christian women—Prayers and devotions. I. Title.
    BV4596.N44B64 2011
    242'.68—dc23   2011020364

Unless otherwise indicated, Scripture quotations are from God's Word®. © 1995 God's Word to the Nations. Used by permission of Baker Publishing Group.

Scripture quotations labeled NIV are from the Holy Bible, New International Version®. NIV®. Copyright © 1973, 1978, 1984, 2010 by Biblica, Inc.™ Used by permission of Zondervan. All rights reserved worldwide. www.zondervan.com

Published in association with the literary agency Books & Such, 52 Mission Circle #122 PMB 170, Santa Rosa, CA 95409.

11   12   13   14   15   16   17   7   6   5   4   3   2   1

Contents

Acknowledgments

To produce this book, I had the help of many eager hands. With my love and thanks to . . .

my husband, Rod, for understanding my need to put knitting before laundry or grocery shopping.

my son, Zach, for waiting until the end of the row with patience.

my agent, Janet Kobobel Grant, for taking me on and turning my hobby into a career.

my editor, Vicki Crumpton, for answering every question with speed and clarity.

my marketing mavin, Janelle Mahlmann, for her expertise given with a smile.

my writing group for good criticism: Ethel Herr, Sherry Cox, Laurie Neurmic, Carol Nicolet Loewen, and Wanda Puder.

my Dream Team for their prayer support and encouragement: Helen Mickelson, Nancy Alfano, Marie Bogart, Terri Torke, Wendy LeClaire, Kelly Schmitt, Linda Bixby, Zanne Dailey, Katie Kerns, Rebecca Petersen, Denise Cooper, Coralie Bokman, Mimi Moseley, Dana Freedman, Eliana Ely, Keli Dericks, Anke Betic, Barb Stewart, Marianne Shine, and Jane Baker.

and to all the knitters who shared their stories. What an inspiration. I want to gather you all in one big circle and knit!

She selects wool and flax
   and works with eager hands. . . .
She opens her arms to the poor
   and extends her hands to the needy.

Proverbs 31:13, 20 NIV

1

Cast On

Beginnings

Cast on: the process of putting stitches on the needle to begin your work.

Knitting can't feed the hungry, fight crime, or stop global warming. But a hand-knit sweater warms a cold child. A cozy scarf eases a homeless night. A tiny hat comforts a preemie head. A lovely prayer shawl wraps a worried patient in peace. Knitting quietly eases some of the hurts in the world. God needs eager knitters to supply these comforts.

Proverbs 31:13 describes a woman eager to work with her hands. To be eager is to have a keen desire or impatient longing. This describes me with my keen desire to have yarn in hand and needles in motion. Did God put the impatient longing in my hands? Can I use this skill for him? I wonder . . .

Knitting brings joy to my world. I get excited about new projects that spark my creativity. When knitting in a group, I enjoy the friendship of others. I bring comfort with items made for charity. Time alone while knitting gives me space to think and pray. The rhythm of yarn moving over needles reduces my stress and helps me relax. It turns out I am not the only one enjoying these knitting pleasures. Many others have stories to tell about woolen wonders in their world, and you will find some of their stories in this book.

Knitting is a gift to rejoice in. Just knit in public, and you'll see how many people are amazed by your skill. It looks quite magical to the mystified. You are likely to hear the comment, "I could never do that!" Pause just a moment to realize how special your talent is. What a gift to have the patience, creativity, and love to knit. Many benefits and pleasures are connected to the craft.

While not a particularly difficult skill to acquire, knitting does take some finesse to do well. It's a talent to cultivate. We all possess a variety of talents, and each one can be used to the glory of God, even doing the laundry! (Read "God's Socks" on page 26 and you'll see what I mean.) These gifts from God are ours to enjoy. The skills we've been given are the perfect set for doing what he has in mind for us: "'For I know the plans I have for you,' declares the LORD, 'plans to prosper you and not to harm you, plans to give you hope and a future'" (Jer. 29:11 NIV). A variety of talents will be needed over your lifetime.

In these pages, you'll find all kinds of knitting stories and information. Friendships, charity knitting, benefits, tips, and how-tos—it's all here. There are tales to inspire and encourage you, as well as a few just to make you smile. The one thing all this has in common is joy. Knitting brings blessings to both sides of the needles, the creator and the receiver.

Do you have a keen desire to discover how to use your talents, to figure out what God wants from you? I wanted to use my talents in big ways for God. I looked for important places to contribute. I tried to find the right committee, organization, or charity. I didn't find a good match.

Then I looked at what filled my life already. I discovered my strengths in simple yet vital tasks. Smiling, cooking, raising my son. Running my home, volunteering at school, attending a Bible study. Knitting. These are small talents by worldly standards, yet when used with the purpose of giving glory to God, they matter the most. What we think is insignificant has a lasting impact.

Is your world filled with needs you may overlook while searching for the next big contribution you can make? Do you wonder how to use the talents you have? Maybe it's time to find new meaning and opportunities in something you're already eager to do.

2

Place a Marker

Aha Moments

Place a marker: putting a plastic ring marker in your work to note a design change or to keep track of the number of stitches.

Some knitting is the get-it-done kind, like mending a sock. Then there are the disaster projects: twenty colors of a fair-isle pattern all tangled in a clump. *What was I thinking?* But for me the majority of knitting is great fun; endless rows of any kind put my mind at ease. I relax, take a breath, and enjoy the rhythm. Knitting provides time for me to think, plan, and pray. Sometimes I find an answer to a question that's been bugging me. Other times I have an "aha moment," those occasions when God gets my attention and plants a seed of insight in my mind. I drop my needles and jot down a new thought.

This chapter is a collection of those aha moments. These are the times I placed a marker to remember a thought that helped build my faith. Each entry in this chapter contains a Bible verse so you too can place a marker and return for new insights. Hopefully you'll find an inspiration here to weave into your own knitting life.

This Doesn't Look Right

Now faith is confidence in what we hope for and assurance about what we do not see.

Hebrews 11:1 NIV

I learned to knit as a teenager. The local library offered a class. Like any beginner, I was all thumbs. The movements didn't feel natural, and they didn't make sense. I wanted beautiful, even stitches, but my work was all bumps. The teacher passed by. "You're doing fine. Keep going." *This is a mess. It can't be right.* The picture in my mind didn't match the rows on my needle. I knit every row just as instructed, but where there should have been lovely stitches, I saw only lumps. In my mind I pictured the distinctive Vs of the stockinette stitch, but I produced the rickrack bumps of the garter stitch.

Has this ever happened to you? In your mind's eye you see one picture, but reality looks very different. The Christian life is "supposed" to be peaches and cream, smooth sailing, no worries, and any other happy cliché you can imagine. The reality is quite different. When you become a Christian, sometimes little on the outside changes: you still have hassles, responsibilities, and chores. But on the inside there's a huge difference. You have faith. You know God is with you.

My first piece of knitting, rows and rows of garter stitches, turned out to be a long, orange snake. We sewed our flat piece into a tube and then stuffed it with plastic bread bags. From the beginning, the piece was supposed to be a snake; I just didn't see it. Looking at my life one row at a time, I can't see how it's all going to turn out. However, God has a plan for me. Even with all the decreases and cable twists, a plan is unfolding. He and I stitch it together one row at a time. Even if sometimes it doesn't look right to me, I know God is with me and sees the end result.

I'll Let You Know

> May God, the source of hope, fill you with joy and peace through your faith in him. Then you will overflow with hope by the power of the Holy Spirit.
>
> Romans 15:13

The first time Marlene taught the Baby Surprise Jacket, the classic Elizabeth Zimmerman design, she got a surprise of her own. She carefully laid out the directions for her students. She assigned knitting to be completed by each class meeting. But she didn't count on anyone racing ahead. At the third class, she discovered several students had interpreted the directions on their own. The beauty of the surprise jacket, at least the first time you make it, is watching this odd piece of material fold into a jacket. The unique construction is the surprise. It is clever and not what a knitter expects.

Marlene had organized her instructions in an orderly step-by-step fashion, but when her students rushed ahead, they made mistakes and had to unravel their projects. Some whined. Marlene wanted to say, "Hey, I was going to show you how to do it if you'd been patient." Of course she held her tongue and gently showed her students how to fix their work.

The second time Marlene taught the Baby Surprise Jacket, her students were on a need-to-know basis. She gave them only the pattern bits they would need to complete the assignment one week at a time. At the last class meeting, she handed them the final directions so they could finish the jacket.

I know how Marlene's first students felt. Sometimes I get so excited that I want to rush ahead and see how things are going to turn out. Sometimes I press on because I want to show off. *See, I know what I'm doing; I don't need your help.* And then just like those knitters, I am surprised when my attempts don't turn out right and I have to backtrack. I do this with more than just knitting. I push on with pursuits in my life, trusting my own understanding. I don't hesitate for reflection or bother with prayer.

If I paused long enough to ask God for help, I would find he has the instructions in hand and will give them to me if I ask. I don't. I make mistakes. I bungle and backtrack and finally ask for help. Sometimes God finds that it works better to give me guidance on a need-to-know basis. He sees me rush ahead and knows I'll do it again. He has the big picture in mind, and I am on the ground with no view of the whole. I think I see what is going on, but clearly his view is better. He has planned an outcome if I follow. I want to see what he sees, and trusting him is maddening sometimes. I cannot see *why* sometimes. I want my own timing. But my way of doing things will not accomplish the big picture the way his timing will. It's hard to focus on the end when being in the middle is so difficult. But I am trying to trust more and more with baby steps.

Frustrated with My Stash

> Pray in the Spirit in every situation. Use every kind of prayer and request there is. For the same reason be alert. Use every kind of effort and make every kind of request for all of God's people.
>
> Ephesians 6:18

I sorted through my stash today, trying to make sense of all the purchases I've made over the years. Yarn to make a Christmas wreath, no knitting required, and I still haven't made it. Stuff to make another bathroom rug. The first one was such fun that I decided to stock up and make several more. Ha. Dark sock yarn for all the men on my list too afraid to wear cool hand-dyed colors. And all this primary-colored, machine-washable wool I planned to use for charity sweaters. It's fun playing with color when making those. I just know a child somewhere will love a festive warm sweater.

There's more. I find afghan amounts of yarn for Warm Up America! squares, and sweater quantities of yarn to knit up, and sock yarn in all my favorite colors—the entire rainbow. I moan. *So much yarn and so little time.* I have the urge to put everything on the needles right now. Cast on and race to the end of each inviting project. It's not just the yarn calling; it's the recipient. I think of all my good intentions. I remember buying the yarn for most of these projects, the excitement of coming home eager to start. Of course I got busy. I may knit every day, but laundry and cooking and living crowd into my needle time.

So as I organized my stash of yarn today, I took the time to pray for the ones I long to give knitted gifts. I thought of cousins and friends. I remembered children in countries I'll never visit. I began to see the reason I was frustrated with my stash: I pray while I knit, and I felt I'd shortchanged everyone I'd wanted to pray for. I took the time to look at each project and pray for the people who may one day see it completed. I smiled. I may never get to all these good intentions, but I can pray for these people anytime I open my closet and look through my drawers of yarn. I tucked my stash back in the closet. This yarn will keep me warm inside for a long time even if I never knit another skein.

Let Me Show You

> Also pray that God will give me the right words to say. Then I
> will speak boldly when I reveal the mystery of the Good News.
>
> Ephesians 6:19

The directions for working the kitchener stitch were laid out on the paper in front of me. I tried to follow along. "Knit remove. Purl don't remove." *Huh?* I should have enough knitting experience to get this; why can't I follow these directions? Finally, I went to a favorite knitting shop and asked for help. "I surrender. I'm waving the white flag. This toe-grafting business is beyond me."

The shop owner smiled. "I still have to look at the directions myself when I do the toe." I cheered a little knowing an expert still needed a little help. We sat down together. She threaded my tapestry needle and handed me the knitting. "Okay. Deep breath. First, on the back needle . . ." And slowly she talked me through the stitch—her calm voice reading each step, my nervous hands executing each maneuver, and her patient eyes watching me as I worked. All became clear. It made so much sense, doing it together.

I love the hands-on part of knitting, the way it is passed on from one to another in person. The fact is, for me, it's easier to understand when I see a new technique done rather than to read about it in a book or follow along online. I like to have a person sitting next to me showing me the way. And this is how it has been for decades. In cozy community, people sit, heads bent over needles, passing on the art of knitting. What a gentle way to learn. I think maybe this is the best way to pass along important information. When the content is vital, it's time to slow down and let it sink in. Sitting side by side, we focus.

I think this must be the very intimate way the gospel was shared in the beginning. One family member to another. One friend to another. One town to another. The Good News sinking in and moving throughout the world. St. Francis of Assisi captured this thought beautifully when he said, "Preach the gospel everywhere you go, and, if necessary, use words." The Good News is a hands-on experience. You can share it intimately with someone seated by your side. Sharing a new craft skill or holding hands in prayer—both are acts of loving-kindness.

Cable Mysteries

> Take these words of mine to heart and keep them in mind. Write them down, tie them around your wrist, and wear them as headbands as a reminder. Teach them to your children, and talk about them when you're at home or away, when you lie down or get up.
>
> Deuteronomy 11:18–19

The cable pattern for the cardigan sweater had an eight-row repeat, only twenty-four stitches wide and running up the front of the sweater. I carefully looked at the chart each time I came to the cable section of the row. I glanced for reassurance every four stitches, making sure I got it right. It took me a long time to get through the first eight rows so I could begin to see the twists taking shape. *What a time-consuming project!* Still, it was my first time cabling, and it was exciting. Experienced knitters told me I'd memorize the pattern in time. *Ha! I doubt it.*

Purl, knit. Purl, knit. The first two and last two stitches of the pattern were always the same. I committed that much to memory. As I worked, I discovered that all even rows were just purling or knitting the stitches as they appeared. I'd memorized half the pattern without even thinking about it. Still, I double-checked the chart every odd-numbered row to make sure my cables were turning in the right direction.

It was slow going, but I delighted in the way the project was turning out. Thirty-six inches of cabling provides an ample number of pattern repetitions. Soon I only peeked at odd-numbered rows. Eventually, I discovered a pattern to this as well. Finally, I just kept track of the row number in my head, knowing what to do. I had memorized the pattern. Unbelievable. The beauty of the mathematical cable twists revealed itself to me. I "got it."

If I could memorize this complicated cabling, why did I struggle committing Bible verses to memory? I never remembered which book, which chapter, and the right verse. I was moaning about this fact to a girlfriend one day. She surprised me by saying, "Those numbers are just there for our convenience; you have the verse in your heart." *Huh?* "You can tell me all kinds of verses from the Bible," she said.

She was right. I have many Scripture passages in my heart, and even a few I can call up by chapter and verse. *When did that happen?* I wondered. Don't I always have to check the pattern, look it up? Sunday school poured many verses into my head when I was little. As an adult I returned to Bible study with a more serious intent. I wanted to learn from God's Word, not just hear the stories. Many of the verses I learned as a child were stuck in my memory already. The first bit of the pattern was embedded.

I stretch to read more and study the Bible. Amazingly, sometimes I manage to commit verses to memory. I call on them in times of stress or joy. Just like the daunting cable pattern I was sure I'd never memorize, through repetition I have put many Bible verses in my heart to stay. The beauty of God's pattern is revealed to me. Joy!

Sweater for the New Baby

> But Mary treasured up all these things and pondered them in her heart.
>
> Luke 2:19 NIV

"I'm with child." Even the whisper of a new baby arriving sends a knitter racing for her needles. When Mary was pregnant with the Christ child, there was probably a lot of whispering going on. So much joy and confusion all wrapped in one simple fact. I thought about this one Christmas season.

Our church planned an Advent art show. A request went out in October for artists to produce a new work honoring the coming of Christ. A photographer, an oil painter, and a poet signed up to work on the project. I wanted to participate, but I felt my crafting could not compete with those fine art offerings. Then it struck me: we are welcoming a baby. And that baby, just like any other, will need warm clothes and soft blankets. I called the coordinator of the show and told her my idea: welcoming the Christ child with a brand-new sweater. She encouraged me to get started.

Knowing the child was a boy, I chose two strong blues and a warm gray color and planned out an argyle design for the front of the sweater. I used the *Guideposts* Knit for Kids pattern as a starting point. (Read more about *Guideposts* on page 94.)

As I knit, I thought of Mary. I kept a verse from Luke in mind. "But Mary treasured up all these things and pondered them in her heart" (2:19 NIV). Moms new and old carry many prayers, wishes, and worries for their children. Mary, I'm sure, was no different. With my thoughts centered on the Christ child, I knit my prayers of peace and love in each row.

As the art show grew closer, I knit faster. Quickly the first Sunday of Advent arrived, and the show was mounted and ready for viewing. Each artist wrote about his or her contribution, and the sentiments were placed on lovely cards hung by the artwork. This is what my card said:

We celebrate the coming of the Christ, who humbled himself to be born an infant Savior. Every newborn needs warm clothes. Our Lord was no different. Initially wrapped in swaddling clothes, Jesus grew into a toddler needing play clothes. No doubt Mary prepared for her son by getting garments ready.

*Knit with love, this tiny sweater honors the coming of the Christ child. When our Advent show is over, this sweater will be sent to **Guideposts** Knit for Kids, who will make sure a child in need receives it.*

God's Socks

> The king will answer them, "I can guarantee this truth: What-ever you did for one of my brothers or sisters, no matter how unimportant they seemed, you did for me."
>
> Matthew 25:40

Offer it up. I had a Catholic upbringing. Whenever I complained about doing chores or homework, my dad told me to "offer it up." I had no idea what he meant. Offer what up? To whom? And how?

Now I'm grown, and I've discovered what my dad meant. Offer the sacrifice of my service up to God as a prayer. I get it. My work, even my chores, can be done in an attitude of joyful prayer and service.

Today, as I sorted the laundry and complained to myself, I heard Dad's voice in my head. "Offer it up." I smiled. I will. I'll offer God the sacrifice of my time to do this chore. If Jesus were here in the flesh, he would need clean socks and fresh sheets just like my family does. I measured the soap, adjusted the dials, and started the next load. I did it with a smile. This service I give my family to keep them comfortable and clean.

My attitude changed. All around me I saw service to offer up with joy. Keeping in touch with friends. Helping a child with homework. Fetching coffee for a co-worker. Knitting a scarf for the homeless. Vacuuming the living room. Life is full of simple tasks we can do with an attitude of happy service rather than race through to get on with the "real" work of the kingdom.

"Whatever you do for one of my brothers, you do for me."
Wow! Thinking of chores this way, it is a privilege to be of
service. Today, I offered up my laundry.

No Time to Knit

> Do not hold back anything good from those who are entitled
> to it when you have the power to do so. When you have the
> good thing with you, do not tell your neighbor, "Go away!
> Come back tomorrow. I'll give you something then."
>
> Proverbs 3:27–28

At the risk of sounding like a Hallmark commercial, let
me say that a simple card really does brighten a person's
day. When there is no time to knit for everyone you'd like
to wrap in comfort, bridge the distance with mail. Email is
great to a point, but having a card you can hold and reread is
so comforting. When was the last time you got friendly mail
from the US postal service? So long ago it's special, I'll bet.

Connecting by mail takes a little extra time. People will
know you went to a little trouble to think of them. When life
gets tough, it's comforting to know others care. Surgeries,
job loss, accidents—all kinds of things scream for a note
of loving-kindness. And I like to send cards long after it's
necessary. The friend recovering from surgery. The widow
still grieving. With the initial news of these situations, cards,
prayers, and food flood the sufferer. But as the rest of the
world gets back to its routine, these people are often left to
heal alone. Two, three, ten months down the road they are still
hurting and wanting a connection with family and friends,

and we often forget them. While the need is fresh, I stockpile an abundance of cards. I keep the stack in a prominent place. Then I am sure to have a card to send off when I think of the person. It could be once a week or every other day—whenever that person comes to mind and I feel the tug to connect.

But what will I say? you wonder. Simply say, "I love you." Or play "remember when," bringing up a happy memory you share together. When sending cards to someone who is in a long recovery period, I send encouragement for sure, but sometimes I send cards acknowledging the pain. "I know you are having some hard days. I am still thinking of you." It's a comfort to know someone realizes they are still in a hard place. Of course, the easiest thing to send is a funny card, a silly picture, or a funny thought. Just sign your name to it and offer your love. For a moment they will be surrounded by joy.

When you don't have the time to knit for every loved one you want to comfort, stop by the card store and pick up a few cards to send. Little joys—our days are made up of these, not grandiose gestures.

No Way to Say Thank You

However, when God our Savior made his kindness and love for humanity appear, he saved us, but not because of anything we had done to gain his approval. Instead, because of his mercy he saved us through the washing in which the Holy Spirit gives us new birth and renewal. God poured a generous amount of the Spirit on us through Jesus Christ our Savior.

Titus 3:4–6

I tour the San Francisco Bay area speaking to MOPS (Mothers of Preschoolers) groups. I enjoy it very much. It is a lot of driving, though, and sometimes I get weary.

One morning I collected the mail. Mostly junk mail as usual. I pulled out a letter with no return address and penned in an unfamiliar hand. The postmark was from Oakland. Intrigued, I opened the note, and a gas gift card fell out. Now I really wondered what was going on. I read the card. It was from a mom who had recently heard me speak at MOPS. She wrote, "Sometimes the most thoughtful people are inadvertently neglected. We all need unexpected kind gestures." Stunned, I smiled. Wow! What a delight. The gas cash was nice, but the bigger "warm fuzzy" was feeling noticed and appreciated.

My very next thought was I need to say thank you. I want to tell this mom what her kind gesture meant to me. But there was no way to find her, no way to say thank you, and it made me a little sad.

It occurred to me that there is another far bigger kindness for which I can never say thank you. Jesus died for me. I do not mean to belittle his great sacrifice by comparing it to an anonymous card, but I was struck by the same feeling. I can never say thank you. Just as the anonymous mom asked for nothing in return, neither does God. He saved me and wants me only to believe and live with that glorious thought and to pass on the knowledge of him to others. It's overwhelming.

The knitting we do for others, especially when we send our stitches to charities far from home, offers selfless lovingkindness. Whether the recipients know Jesus Christ or not, our gift is an act they will remember. Our knitted items may be the very thing to plant a seed of faith. They may want to say thank you one day, as I wanted to, but the only way to say how blessed they feel is to tell others of their experience and give all the credit to God.

Woolen Legacy

> Train a child in the way he should go, and even when he is old he will not turn away from it.
>
> Proverbs 22:6

When my grammy Mabel went to heaven, her death was not unexpected. She was 101 years old. A century of living. I began to wonder, *What did she leave behind? What is her legacy?* The thought stuck with me for days as I got ready to attend Mabel's memorial.

Gram lived in Wisconsin. I live in Northern California. I had to make travel plans for December in Wisconsin. It was going to be very cold, and I did not own a winter coat.

I stood in Macy's for forty-five minutes trying on coats. Faux fur. Shawl collars. Tweeds. Even sheep skin. I shrugged off coat after coat, frustrated. I knew I needed real wool to keep me warm; any synthetic would let the Wisconsin cold through to my bones. How did I know? I knew because I watched my gram scrutinize the label of every coat she ever saw. We used to tease her and call her Label Conscious Mabel. She loved coats and owned many; they were all top quality. Mabel had a little cottage industry as a seamstress, so she knew how to spot quality.

30

When I was younger and the latest style mattered more than a classic look, I used to get annoyed with Gram when she would bend back the collar of my coat (while I was wearing it!). She would tsk-tsk at the no-name low quality of my choice. Standing in Macy's, I grinned in the mirror at the coat I modeled. It was a Kenneth Cole made of 100 percent fine black merino wool. Grammy would approve.

The qualities of a product are displayed on the label. Not all labels are as easily read as the tag on a coat. Outward appearances can be deceptive. It may look like fine wool, but the tag tells you it's 70 percent acrylic and 30 percent nylon. No warmth there. Outward appearances may show the trappings of fine character, but a look below the surface reveals a checkbook with no charitable contributions, subscriptions to questionable publications, and other paper trails showing a selfish life.

I want my label to read:

> *Christian: 100% product of grace*
> *Living to carry the torch to the next generation*

I think that's the label you'd find on Mabel's life. She believed. She took it on faith. We are a family of strong Scandinavian stock, sometimes stoic but deeply loving and faithful. Ours is not a family that talks about the Lord and what he has done in our lives. It sounds foreign on my tongue to say aloud, "Jesus saved me." Yet I deeply believe it and have a strong faith. It's a faith given to me as a child that blossomed in adulthood. My parents told me the Christian story. They heard the Good News from their parents, who heard the Word from their parents.

Of the many memories I hold of my grammy Mabel, the most important one is her legacy of faith. It was not spoken of so much as lived out. Mabel was certain of the story, and she passed it on. Now she's living out the eternal chapter. Hers is a wonderful legacy of faith. What kind of legacy are you building and passing on? Sharing your craft and life with others is a strong legacy.

Speak the Language

The tongues of wise people give good expression to knowledge, but the mouths of fools pour out a flood of stupidity. . . . A soothing tongue is a tree of life, but a deceitful tongue breaks the spirit.

Proverbs 15:2, 4

Every profession, hobby, or specialized pursuit speaks a language all its own. Football players speak in a different dialect than cattle ranchers. Oncologists talk in terms foreign to watchmakers. Even mommies of preschoolers speak differently than moms of teenagers. Knitters communicate in a jargon all their own too. At my house we call it "knittish." Terms start in general: yarn is soft or fluffy, scratchy or acrylic. Then things get more specific as we talk worsted, mohair, gauge, and purl. Even the needles have specific names: double pointed, cable, and tapestry. And when you begin to read a pattern, it turns to alphabet soup: k2, p2, yo, ssk, M1, sl. What does all this mean?

Speak the lingo of a hobby, profession, or pursuit, and you possess the secret knowledge. With a level of understanding, you use the shorthand to go deeper into the subject and learn more from others. Yet the very jargon that connects you to experienced knitters can exclude someone just beginning.

When you speak an exclusive language, others don't get it. Learning a new vocabulary is difficult. We do this as Christians. We have shorthand, "Christianese," that confounds others. Saved, born again, seeker, put it on my heart, in this season, the Lord moved—the list goes on and on. All we are really trying to communicate is how much God loves us and we in return love him. The hurdle of language gets in our way. Rather than draw people in, we might keep them at arm's length.

If you tell a new knitter to knit two together, yarn over, you will get a blank stare. The same barrier goes up if you launch into apologetics with someone who doesn't speak Christianese. And even worse, they may tune you out immediately. "The Lord told me . . ." Suddenly there's a blank stare. If you want to help a new knitter get more comfortable with the lingo, explain as you go and show, don't tell. Speak an inclusive language. If you want to share your faith, speak plainly the language of love.

Better Than a Sale on Cashmere

I didn't speak my message with persuasive intellectual arguments. I spoke my message with a show of spiritual power so that your faith would not be based on human wisdom but on God's power.

1 Corinthians 2:4–5

"What are you making?"

It's the opening every knitter expects. It's time to show off your latest project. A chat about where you found the yarn and the pattern may follow. You might end up discussing whom the item is for, how long you've been working on it, and when you hope to finish. Often a stranger gets more information about your knitting project than she intended to receive. And if you are talking to a fellow knitter, the discussion goes on and on as the two of you are united in a love of the craft.

Knitters share tips and compliments all the time. We collect patterns and yarn and new knitting buddies. It dawned on me recently that I don't talk about the gospel with as much enthusiasm as I do knitting. I am quick to say, "I love this yarn," or ask, "Where did you get that pattern?" I take more pleasure in chatting about fibers than I do in telling someone, "Hey, God loves you. In fact, God loves you so much that he died to save you, and now he wants to live in your heart."

The Good News is far better than a sale on cashmere, and yet I get more excited with loose threads. It's hard for me to talk about my love of God; I get tongue-tied. Maybe the thing to do is share the Good News around the knitting circle. Then the deeds I do will give wings to my words. The next time I'm asked, "What are you making?" I can tell them about the joy I find in sharing my craft with those in need. I'll tell them about the little sweaters I knit to show the love of

God to children half a world away whom I will never meet. Now that's a conversation starter.

———

Now with hearts ready and needles waiting, let's look at what some other knitters have been up to. There are friends to meet along the way. The next chapter will introduce you to some lovely knitters enjoying their craft together.

3

Knit Two Together

Friendship

Knit two together: knitting two stitches together to make one. Common abbreviation k2tog.

Stronger than any felted bag, more powerful than a sale on cashmere—these are the bonds knitters forge. Knitters are friendly, patient people. Who else could find humor in ripping out a sleeve for the third time to get it right? And who else but a knitter is going to understand? We need each other to share the thrills and frustrations of the craft. And we love a good story. The first thing most knitters ask each other is,

"What are you working on?" That opening leads to some interesting tales. Friendships beginning with the love of yarn grow deeper over time as we share more than just our latest knitting triumphs. I've gathered some stories here to celebrate both the gift of knitting and the friends we find and share through the craft.

The Knitting Niece

It started out as an annual trip to the Knitting Guild of America's Summer Show. It grew into a special time for aunt and niece that almost preempted a wedding.

Marlene Reilly told me about nurturing her niece Andrea's knitting skills. Here is her story.

"Andrea and I have been knitting together since she was in her teens. We go to the Knitting Guild of America's show every summer. We've followed the show to stops all over the East Coast. We've been from Philadelphia, Pennsylvania, to Manchester, New Hampshire. Every year we'd get our knit fix with classes, fibers, and a general overload on all things knitted. But there was never much time to actually knit. So we started having weeklong knit vacations. Andrea would come for a visit, and we'd launch into her latest knitting whim. One year she wanted to try felted clogs. She was thrilled with the results. The best year, though, was the year of the Icelandic sweaters.

"Andrea announced that she wanted to try an Icelandic knit but didn't quite have the nerve. She had never tried stranded work but loved the look of those intricate patterns. 'No problem,' I told her. 'You could knit one of those in a week.' With her growing expertise and patience, I knew she could do it. And that's what we set out to do. We scheduled a week's vacation. First, we went yarn shopping. I was conservative and picked out some grays and a blue. Andrea chose greens and white. Next, we picked up our favorite munchies and chick flicks for the week.

"We knit for over eleven hours a day. Most days we didn't even get out of our pajamas. It was all about the yarn and the next row. Late afternoon would roll around, and we'd realize it would be dinnertime soon. We'd have to decide where to order takeout. My husband would come home and see the state of affairs. He didn't mind. He'd seen this kind of yarn frenzy before. Still, he didn't quite understand the thrilled but dazed look in our eyes as we got closer to the finish line.

"I did schedule a break in the week. One evening I drove Andrea into New York City to see *Wicked* on Broadway. Of course, Andrea brought her knitting along, taking advantage of the commute time. We even wondered for a moment if we should hide the knitting in the trunk. We didn't want someone to steal her awesome creation so near completion. You can see we were a little crazed at that point. And, yes, we did complete our sweaters in a week. Best knit vacation ever!"

In 2009, the Knitting Guild of America's Summer Show was in Buffalo, New York, over the weekend of August 8. It seems the organizers could not be persuaded to move festivities to accommodate Andrea's wedding that weekend, though she did ask politely a year in advance. Marlene and Andrea paused, but for only a moment. There would be other shows. This year the fond memory was a happy aunt watching a favorite niece get married to a husband who, like hers, understood the need for a spare room full of yarn and the nonnegotiable annual week off for knitting.

The Yarn-Yarn Sisterhood

Back in 2003, Michelle Murray asked Terri Smith to knit a chemo cap. Michelle wanted to make caps for cancer patients, and she was looking for knitters to join her efforts. She knew Terri from church and discovered she was a knitter too. "Would you make a chemo cap?" Terri was a knitter, but she had never knit a hat before. She was willing to try. "Sure. How do I do that?"

"My mom was my knitting mentor," Terri says. "I learned to knit when I was little, but Mom always cast on for me even as a grown woman. When I ran into problems, she fixed them. I never learned how to troubleshoot my knitting. She took my work and made it right. Once I was trying to learn something out of a book and could not understand the directions. The left-handed instructions didn't make any sense. I asked my mom about it.

"'Terri, you don't knit left-handed,' she said.

"'But I'm left-handed, and so are you.'

"'True, but my mom was right-handed and taught me to knit right-handed. So I taught you the same way.'"

Terri laughs. "Crazy huh? When my mom passed away from breast cancer, I couldn't knit—too many memories of working on our projects together. I put down my needles for over two years. Then Michelle asked me to make a chemo cap. It felt like the right time to knit again."

Michelle was expanding her knit knowledge too. In 2001, when her sister announced she was going to have a baby, Michelle went to the local yarn shop and selected supplies for a crochet baby blanket. She admired some of the knitted creations there and decided to learn to knit instead. Of course, that was the beginning of a new fiber hobby. Michelle is always intrigued by the "artistically interesting" as she calls it. The day I met Michelle she had just come from a glass-blowing session. Her interest in the arts is not limited to yarn, but fibers are a favorite. Michelle tithes her knitting time. She once added up all the hours she spent knitting in one week. Now she tries to spend 10 percent of her knitting time on charity projects. "All knitting time is fun, but this gives it a purpose as well."

So Michelle and Terri knit chemo caps and discovered a lovely friendship. They began to share their knitting knowledge with each other. Terri says, "Mom taught me to work with quality supplies. Cheap yarn is not soothing. Mom used to say, 'Good materials will help you feel successful.' That and your project will be gorgeous."

Michelle continued to offer Terri help after their cap project. As Terri tells it, "I gave Michelle a copy of a recent pattern I was working on, so when I called her for help she was ready."

Michelle is quick to point out that Terri offers her help too. "I was going through a tough time and became completely convinced God did not love me. One lousy afternoon Terri happened to call, and she could tell something was wrong. I decided to tell her how I was really feeling. It was such a relief to talk to someone about it."

Terri remembers that day. "One of my gifts is faith. It is a solid thing I never even question. It's my spiritual gift. So talking to Michelle has given me such empathy for those who struggle with faith issues. It's helped both of us."

Michelle and Terri are working on sharing their friendship with others at their church. Through women's ministry they are starting a weekly knit group, the Yarn-Yarn Sisterhood. Michelle and Terri know the happiness of a yarn friend, and they want others to find the same thing.

The Knitting Retreat

"Sign-ups started today. You'd better grab a spot!" The South Bay Knitters escape annually to knit. They used to plan a retreat twice a year, summer and winter, but heat and mosquitoes ruled out July as an ideal knitting month. However, the first weekend in January still goes on the calendar every year. The thirty spots fill up fast, and the wait list begins.

The South Bay Knitters started over twenty years ago. The monthly meetings were such fun that it was a natural progression for someone to think an entire weekend of knitting would be even better. The weekend is all knitting all the time. There are no vendors or sales; the only agenda is friendship. During the first retreat, eight knitters spent a weekend knitting in Big Sur. It was great fun but a little pricey. Catie Kniess took on the challenge of finding another spot for the group.

Catie located a retreat center for the group to rent. It's not fancy, but the setting is lovely, in the redwoods of the Santa Cruz Mountains. The knitters share small guest rooms and a common bath. After their first year, the knitters "demanded" hiring a chef and a cleanup crew. No sense wasting any knit time whatsoever. This adds a little to the cost but is well worth the expense and added level of pampering. This group does not want to waste time with meal interruptions either, so they have honed the schedule to include only brunch and dinner. The chef sets out fresh scones for the early risers, and the knitters provide snacks for all-day grazing. Meals are covered, and no knit time is lost. The rest of the day is simple: they gather in the main meeting room, stoke up the fireplace, and settle in for fun, knitting, and conversation. Some take a break to go for a hike in the redwoods or to do yoga. A few years ago they started hiring a masseuse. And while it is another expense, sign-ups for her time are as coveted as spots at the retreat itself.

January 2010 was the eleventh year for this retreat. The old guard signed up in a hurry. But there was room for eight to ten day trippers, knitters coming in for just Saturday. I can tell you from experience that this group is very welcoming to newcomers. I was a little nervous jumping into a group not knowing a soul. I didn't need to worry. Knitters enjoy talking about the craft. What an easy way to get acquainted. At the end of my day with them, I was hugged and invited back the following year.

On Saturday afternoon is the Stealing Gift Exchange. The rules are simple: each person brings a wrapped knitting gift, but nothing tacky. Then each player draws a number. In numerical order they take turns picking a gift or stealing one. Sometimes there is yarn they wish they hadn't purchased or will never get to use. Other times there are patterns and books. Then there was the year of Babs. Babs is the knitting chicken from the movie *Chicken Run*. The gift was an adorable figurine of Babs knitting beak warmers. Babs was such a popular gift that she must have changed hands over fifty times. The women laughed until their sides hurt. The lucky winner finally took Babs to her room for safekeeping. In the morning, though, she found a ransom note left by a couple of her knitting friends. Eventually, Babs was returned unharmed. And her new owner spent the next week online looking for two more Babs figurines to give her kidnappers.

During the retreat, mealtime is the only time everyone sets down their needles. Even while playing the gift game, everyone knits during the proceedings. Each woman is happy to share her latest project and get advice from the group. With the luxury of time, no one has to hurry. Each woman can relax and visit while knitting. No wonder this is an annual escape with a waiting list.

Office Knitting

Knitting at work is commonplace these days. Lunchtime knit groups pop up everywhere. And when there's a pregnant co-worker in the office, it's the best excuse ever to come together and make a few tiny garments. But what about all those proud daddies-to-be who are just as excited? Why not lavish on them a little celebration too? That's just what a friend of mine did in her office.

"'Steve's wife is pregnant!' one of the women in our lunchtime knit group told me. 'Let's knit a baby layette for Steve. He loves camo, and I found this.' She handed me some acrylic camouflage-colored yarn. 'You're in charge of the jacket,' she said. 'I'll do the blanket, and we'll get Susan to do the hat and booties.' This stuff looked terrible to me; still, it would be perfect for Steve. Then an idea sprang to mind. Let's get everyone in the office to help, make it a group effort.

"Being the boss has its privileges. I told everyone in the office to do at least three stitches on the layette project, whether they knew how to knit or not. I stood over several of the men as they fumbled through their paces. Some still thought of knitting as a grandmotherly pursuit. They were surprised at the dexterity needed to make their three stitches. I insisted everyone take a turn. This gift would be from all of us.

"As the project progressed, I heard whispers at my office door: 'How is the sweater going?' All the people who thought knitting was good for nothing suddenly had a vested interest in the project. 'See? Those are my three stitches!' They puffed with pride. It's a powerful feeling creating something with your hands. It was a team-building project like no other, and we didn't even have to pay a corporate consulting guru.

"Oh, and Steve loved our gift."

Working at It

A stray email landed in my husband's mailbox at work. "The knit group will meet this Tuesday in the atrium." *We have a knit group?* He decided to check it out. He went to ask Susan about her email.

"My wife is one of you crazy knitters. Can anyone join your lunch bunch?"

"Sure, we'd love to have her."

"Do you guys talk about work a lot?"

"No, we pretty much keep it to knitting. We need the break."

"Cool. I'll let her know."

The following Tuesday I arrived at noon, knit bag in hand, ready to meet the gang. Sometimes when you are about to meet a new group, the nerves jump in your tummy. Instead, I raced up the steps eager to meet more knitters. These are my kind of folks. Like kids on a playground, we had a common interest.

The first question any knitter asks another is usually, "What are you working on?" Brian showed me his melting soft angora lace scarf. Mike brought out the sweater he was making for his dog. Beth held up the swatch waiting to become a beanie hat. Susan arrived to display the adorable tunic she was finishing for her new niece. I showed them the red sock I was making for my mom's birthday. And that was that.

From then on it was all knit all the time. There were no questions like, "What do you do?" Rather, we swapped websites we loved, traded names of stores we liked to frequent, and asked questions about technique. The entire hour brought the biggest smile to my face. And like a kid on the playground I asked, "Can I play with you guys again next week?" Sure!

I am older than most of the people by five to ten years. It's fun to see their fresh take on knitting. Mike ran into a snag on his doggie sweater when he got to the buttonholes. It was between Tuesdays, when the group could help out, so he went online to find instructions. The buttonholes he displayed the following Tuesday were perfect. We all marveled at them. "I found a video on YouTube. I watched really closely until I got it. I couldn't understand the woman; she was talking in Portuguese."

"You learned this off the web in Portuguese? Unbelievable!"

Mike's take on knitting continued to fascinate me. He jumped in with both feet and knit hard. He's so enthusiastic. When he discovered a yarn he loved, he decided to buy a hank of every color rather than make the difficult decision of which one. "This is the first time I've bought yarn without a project in mind." I smiled at his comment. *Welcome to the dark side, Mike.* I didn't have the heart to tell him it's the beginning of his stash. He'll find out soon enough.

Mike did finally knit a scarf with some of his new acquisition. He decided to make a scarf the long way. He carefully calculated how many stitches to cast on and then knit for miles. When the creation finally came off the needles, he discovered that his calculations had been a tiny bit off. The blocked scarf stretched twelve feet! But, oh, it was gorgeous. The group laughed and also applauded his efforts. "It's a wonderful warm scarf, even if I do have to double it up." We all agreed.

Each Tuesday brings another time to pick up needles in the middle of a busy workweek and meet with friends. It's a delight to have this break in the day. So many projects fly by, and the group grows with new members. It's just the break we need to remind us all what fun it is to have knitting friends.

Secret Knitting

In my family we love a surprise. We even take it to the point of silliness. My mom especially loves to surprise her kids. She knit my older brother a new sweater for every birthday when he was little. Of course, she wanted it to be a secret. The first time really was: she measured him in his sleep! The sweater was a big surprise and fit perfectly.

My aunt used a unique method for her knitting surprise. "I need to take some measurements," she told her daughters. "You girls are the same size as your cousins, so we can make a secret gift for them that will fit just right." The sweaters did fit like a dream. The knitter had actually measured the true receivers. Sneaky.

I gave up on surprise knitting after I made my mom the perfect red sweater for Christmas only to find out I had guessed wrong with the size. The lovely sweater fit my neighbor instead. Don't worry about Mom, though. I got wise and took measurements for the replacement. She received a new red sweater for Valentine's Day instead.

These days when I embark on a special sweater (and so far that has only been for blood relatives), I take the person along for yarn and pattern selection. My deadline is still Christmas, but this way I am not the only one anticipating the outcome. The recipient knows what I am up to. I even call now and then to give an update on my progress. This keeps me going. It's fun to "torture" them with information. *I finished the sleeves and started the back.* We all have fun when it's time to open the gift at Christmas.

My family is not the only one engaging in secret Christmas knitting. I talked to Anne Cutrell, who told me her secret knitting story.

"When I was small, probably seven or eight, my mum started reknitting a sweater for my Dad. It was a beautiful aran sweater, but it was the wrong size, either too big or too small. I don't remember which. She unraveled it and reknit it in the same style, but this time it was the right size. My job was to make sure that when Dad came home the project was out of sight to keep it a surprise. I felt very proud that Mum entrusted me with such an important job. I'm happy to say Dad was very proud when he received the sweater for Christmas—caught completely unawares."

Where Did My Hat Come From?

For many people, the clothes they wear are a mystery. How does fleece become a sweater? There are many steps involved. Shearing the sheep. Washing and carding the fleece. Spinning the wool. Dyeing the fiber. Knitting the pattern. Often all this is taken for granted. They just go to the store and buy what's in fashion at the moment.

When you are three and a half years old, everything in the world is brand-new and needs explanation. Mommies are forever answering the questions Why? How come? Where does it come from? Recently, Ginger Bihm got to show her daughter Sydney where her hat came from and a whole lot more.

Ginger relates the story.

"Over Christmas vacation, my sister-in-law Christy and I took Sydney to the store and let her pick out yarn for a hat that Christy was going to make for her. Sydney also picked out a couple of buttons for the flap on the hat. She chose a doggie button and a kitty button to go with the pink yarn. What a combo, but she's three and a half, and that's what she wanted. We also let her help pick the yarn (multicolored) and button (swirly) for her little sister's hat. Christy knitted both hats during her visit. Sydney saw the yarn gradually turn into a hat. She even tried it on several times as they checked the fit.

"All this started a conversation about clothes and where they come from. 'Yes, that sweater is made of yarn, but it was probably made by a machine and not a person. The yarn comes from cotton that grows in the field.' Aha. I could see the light go on in her head. *So tractors and plowing aren't just for food.* 'This is what a spinning wheel is,' Christy explained. No longer was it just a mysterious and meaningless object from *Sleeping Beauty.* 'Your T-shirt is made of tiny threads, but they are basically the same as yarn.' And on and on it went. We are still having bits of conversation about the entire process. Out of the blue Sydney will say, 'Hey,

Mom, look. My doggie baby [stuffed animal] has skin that is cloth, with fur!' It's all a revelation to her and so fun to watch."

Do you remember your first fiber memory? Who knows when those seeds are planted. Sydney may be an avid knitter someday, not ever knowing when the bug bit her. Even if she never picks up a needle, she has a newfound love for hand-knits. Sydney is sure to receive other such wonderful gifts in her lifetime, for when you value the effort put into a hand-knit, you are more likely to receive one.

No Fear

Knitters think differently about time. I am always surprised when someone asks me how long it takes me to knit something. I just don't measure that time. I know I can knit a sweater in a month or a pair of socks in a weekend, but that's not the point. I don't measure the time in hours; I measure it in quality. Maybe you are the same, always with a project on the needles and counting that time as well spent. Since knit time is time well spent, I was delighted when I got a call from my friend Beth.

"Julia would like to knit with you."

"Really? Sure, that would be fun." Beth is not a knitter, but her daughter Julia, a fifth grader, has been taken with knitting since the second grade. Actually, Julia is into all kinds of crafts. At eleven she is already building her stash and collecting supplies for all her craft interests. She makes cards and beaded jewelry. She goes on eBay to buy supplies and find new gadgets. Beth encourages Julia's creativity even though she's not a crafter at heart herself.

Julia and I made a date. After our first knit session, we decided it would be fun to make it a weekly event when our busy schedules allowed. Since Julia already knew how to knit, I showed her tricks of the trade: weaving in the ends, how to cable, and yarn selection. We had discussions knitters have about finding the right yarn or loving the challenge of an intricate pattern. We had a very pleasant autumn together.

In the spring, Julia wanted to make a pair of socks for her dad's birthday. Socks intimidated me for years before I ever had the nerve to try them. Julia showed no fear, and I was not about to dampen her enthusiasm. I remember being young and grown-ups telling me I could not try a new skill because I was too little. I wanted to put those skills in Julia's hands. Still, I wanted to make sure she was up for the challenge and quizzed her first.

"Have you ever worked in the round?"

"Nope."

"This is more complicated than a scarf. Socks will take a while to complete."

"That's okay."

"They won't be done in time for your dad's birthday in two weeks."

"I can make him a card with a coupon for socks. Then I can knit in front of him and won't have to keep it a secret."

Okay then. Julia was ready. I was the nervous one. Could I really teach her how to knit a pair of socks?

Julia already knit and purled like a pro. The first hurdle was knitting in the round. She picked it up in an afternoon. Assignment #1: knit two purl two round and round until the leg of the sock measures the same as one of your dad's crew socks.

I told my protégé she could call anytime for advice. I'd be happy to stop by for a help session if necessary. When you are young and enthusiastic, there is nothing worse than waiting for a grown-up to have time to help you. A few evenings later my phone rang.

"Lisa, are you busy?"

"What's up?"

"I've made a mistake somewhere. There are more stitches on one needle than the other."

"Well, I'm free after dinner. I'll be over." Knitter in distress; I had to go. Happily, it was an easy fix. Julia was back on track again.

When you are eleven, there are distractions. (Even when you are forty-eight, there are distractions!) Like every other knitter I know, Julia became interested in other projects. Her dad's socks waited as she tried cake decorating, jewelry making, and stationery design. But the weather cooled off and knitting appealed again.

We moved on to the heel and picking up stitches for the gusset. For Julia, each new part of the sock was a knitting adventure, not a trauma. Not knowing that others might have been intimidated, Julia launched into each part of the sock with no fear. I was happy to share the journey with her. I started out thinking I didn't have the teaching skills to pull it off, but joy in the craft helped smooth the way. You'd be surprised how easy it is to teach a willing student. Next time someone asks you to teach them to knit, give it a try. I bet you'll both be pleased with the outcome.

Knitter At-Large

Audrey Fisher is a mobile woman. Her busy schedule keeps her moving around the country. And her family is spread from Oakland to Chicago to Tennessee. So she has many spots she calls home. Audrey is a knitting woman too. This combination, mobile consultant and fiber fiend, makes Audrey a knitter at-large. Audrey talks about her knitting life.

"Every time I get ready to head out, I go online to look up knit shops in the area. I'm often in town for weeks or months, and I can't go without yarn for that long. I like to make a connection to the knitting community wherever I am.

"Yarn shops are friendly places to go. I usually feel so welcomed. I like to sign up for a class I can take after work. Evenings and weekends are best. It's fun when the class meets weekly rather than a one-day deal. I get to know the group that way, and it's more fun. I've taken a lot of designer classes from national visiting teachers. Those are fun, and I have many signed books from authors. But I really like to sit and knit with the same group week to week. I feel more a part of the circle that way. And I meet people from so many different backgrounds.

"I have friends sprinkled all over and many favorite shops: Genuine Purl in Chattanooga, Knitch in Atlanta, Cast On

Cottage in Roswell, Sheepish in Decatur, and Piedmont Yarn and Apparel in Oakland. All these shops have one thing in common: they are so welcoming to their customers. I can go to any one of them for help, and the workers take the time to answer my questions without making me feel dumb. That keeps me coming back for more.

"The other thing these shops have in common is a variety of great yarns. I am learning how important that is. All these great yarns, and they feel so good. I can never go back to acrylic. The other month I was in Chicago and helped my sister, mom, and cousin crochet together a blanket of knit squares as a gift for one of my other cousins. We ran out of yarn and had to head to the bargain store for more. It hurt my hands to work with acrylic.

"Sometimes I buy yarn just to have it. I display it on my dining room table in an eclectic arrangement. People don't know what to say when they see it. They kinda eyeball my table and wonder about me. Then I show them my knitting room. That leaves them speechless. I love yarn.

"When I was little, my grandma and I would get on the train in Oakland and go to Southern California to visit my great aunt. My aunt had one of those big old houses with window seats. When you lifted the lid on the seats, you'd find piles of yarn hidden away. Every evening I sat and learned to knit and crochet. What an experience.

"In 2005, I was diagnosed with MS. This means I have some cognitive and hand issues. I can't always call up the memory of what to do. Knitters are such caring people. I have found many who will answer my knit questions with patience. I sometimes have to ask the same question over and over. It's so nice when I find a place where there are friendly answers rather than impatience.

"My brother-in-law travels to many countries. Lately, he's been sending me yarn from Spain, Denmark, and Paris. My family is about to leave on a trip to Spain. You know I'll be looking for more of that great yarn my brother-in-law found. New yarn is a treat to find, but new knit friends are the best part of my yarn habit."

———

Do these stories help you remember your knitting friendships? I hope so. Every time you see a knitter, you have an instant connection. And knitters have a long history. In the next chapter, we'll find out more about those we are connected to from the past.

4

Continue in Established Pattern

History

Continue in established pattern: to keep knitting with no changes to the pattern as already set in your work.

As a knitter, you are a part of a long line of people making garments and art from yarn. One of the earliest known knitted items dates from the first millennium AD, a pair of finely decorated cotton socks found in Egypt. Our craft connects us to a rich history stretching back thousands of years. In the beginning, necessity meant knitting to clothe the family.

Now many of us have the leisure to share our gift with family and friends, as well as those in need.

When I began to look at the history of knitting, I knew about women knitting socks for the troops during World War II, but I found that knitting history contains many other interesting tidbits. Some of the following stories are about knitters from long ago, and some of the tales come from knitters today who are sharing their histories with us. These stories and others like them helped establish the pattern we continue today: knitting for those we love and those in need.

Thirteen Colonies and One Spy

For me, knitting history brings images of World War II and all those soldiers needing socks. But war relief and charity knitting began much earlier. The Revolutionary War kept Americans knitting. The new nation had no formal army, only local militias. These troops needed all the help they could get. Washington's troops endured harsh conditions, freezing winters, and long marches on muddy roads. Many soldiers wore nothing to cover their feet but rags. The call went out for socks.

All through the colonies, women were urged to help clothe the army. They knit socks and sewed shirts. Rhoda Farrand was a New Jersey woman who answered the plea. The story handed down tells how her husband wrote to her about the soldiers' bleeding feet in Morristown, New Jersey. She enlisted her son Dan to drive her to neighbors to recruit more women. Rhoda organized the women to knit hundreds of warm, woolen stockings. Finally, she delivered the woolens to the men in Morristown herself.[1]

Another revolutionary helped in a very different way. Old Mom Rinker was a knitter who lived near Philadelphia. Tavern keepers eavesdropped on British soldiers and then fed Mom Rinker any information they overheard. Mom Rinker wrote her intelligence on slips of paper and tucked them into her balls of yarn. Then she took her knitting out to the edge of town to sit and work. From high on her hill, the view was lovely, looking over the troops camped below. When soldiers passed below, she'd kick a ball of yarn over the edge. A soldier, sent for this very purpose, would pick up the yarn and deliver it to General Washington. The picture was one of innocence: an old woman knitting and a soldier picking up a ball of yarn. Who would think twice?[2]

The Everyday

History does not often record the mundane. (Of course, YouTube is changing all that.) Knitting nestles in the nooks and crannies of history. Knitting eventually reached the White House. Many of the first ladies knit; it was part of life even in high office. First Lady Ida Saxton McKinley knit hundreds of bedroom slippers for charities, and many were auctioned for fund-raising. Eliza McCardle Johnson, wife of seventeenth president Andrew Johnson, spent much of her time knitting, reading, and visiting with family during her time in the White House.[3]

During the Victorian Era, women spent the bulk of their time at home with family. It was a quiet life but one with purpose. Even in this era of necessity knitting, women did not confine their craft to immediate family. The less fortunate received gifts. Thousands of charity organizations throughout the country produced knitted and sewn items for the poor. These groups also sold their handicrafts to raise money for schools, orphanages, homes for the elderly, soup kitchens, and other worthy causes.

Knitting for North and South

When the American Civil War erupted, knitters in the North and the South rushed to help their boys. Both sides assumed they would achieve a quick victory, but needs mounted as the war dragged on. Knitting became a badge of honor nationwide. Thousands of charities sprang up throughout the country to support the war effort of both armies. The US Sanitary Commission became the central entity to organize the knitted and sewn products of the charities throughout the North. The South did not have a central organization to direct donations. This meant women met in homes and on plantations. They had to scrounge for scarce supplies. They used any fiber available to knit. They even unraveled old garments to make new items.

Hand-knit socks were prized possessions, and the demand was huge. Many of the knitted items arrived with notes of encouragement for the soldiers. "Socks sent home in the knapsack of a dear brother who fell at Antietam." "Stockings knit by a little five-year-old girl, and she's going to knit some more." And this note: "The fortunate owner of these socks is secretly informed that they are the one hundred and ninety-first pair knit for our brave boys by Mrs. Abner Bartlett of Medford, Massachusetts, now 85 years."[4] Mrs. Bartlett was a prolific knitter. She produced more than three hundred pairs of socks. She started knitting in September of 1861. In February of 1865, she sent her three-hundredth pair of socks to President Lincoln.

Many knitters sent items directly to President Lincoln. Ninety-one-year-old Sarah Phelps of Gorton, New Hampshire, sent the president her knitting along with a note of encouragement: "that you might be richley indoued with that wisdom which you have so much kneaded to enable you to bare so grate responsibilities & to do that that is the good for our bleding Country." Another patriot, Lucy Thomas, sent the president hand-knit gloves with this note: "Sir, this pair of Gloves was knit Expressly as a present to your excellency by Mrs. Lucy A. Thomas, widow & relict of the late Hon. Ira Thomas of Adams Jeff Co. N.Y."[5]

The knitting effort needed cash to keep going. To raise money for their cause, organizations in the North sponsored fairs. What began on the local level to raise money soon was taken over by the US Sanitary Commission, who sponsored "Sanitary Fairs" in major cities such as Chicago, New York, and Philadelphia. All manner of things were available for sale, not just knitted items. A lock of General Grant's hair was auctioned off in Rochester, New York. And the Chicago fair boasted the original draft of the Emancipation Proclamation. President Lincoln contributed it with this note: "I desire to retain the paper, but if it shall contribute to the relief and comfort of the soldiers, that will be better."[6]

Knitting for soldiers did not end with the Civil War. World War I and World War II both had knitting campaigns.

World War Knitting

The knitting effort in both world wars is often the first image that comes to mind when discussing knitting history. Millions of items were knit for soldiers and refugees. Wool was as important a resource as steel. In fact, steel knitting needles were considered such a necessity to World War II that they were not collected in scrap-metal drives.

The American Red Cross became synonymous with knitting for the war effort in the United States. During World War I, the Red Cross grew at an extraordinary pace with hundreds of new chapters. Knitters of all ages picked up their needles. The Junior Red Cross was formed during this time as regional schools partnered with the Red Cross to get children knitting for "our boys." The organization became the clearinghouse for all knitted items going to the troops. There were strict guidelines and quality controls. Only items knit with approved patterns and made with white cotton or gray, khaki, or navy wool were allowed.

Knitting was a comfort to both the knitter and the soldier. Those at home had something to do as their worry mounted, and the soldiers of course received physical comforts. Sweaters, vests, helmet covers, and socks were in demand. Socks were most important of all. They wore out from heavy use and needed to be replaced. The hand-knit versions were superior to the machine-made socks of the time. Many knitters made the same item in the same size. This way they memorized the pattern and worked faster.

Those not adept at making socks joined the effort by producing bandages, strips of knitting fifteen to twenty feet long. The garter stitch was ideal for these, since the stitch is stretchy and lies flat. The Red Cross sterilized the bandages and sent them to medical units worldwide.

World War II saw knitters picking up their needles again. It was a natural response for many who had been children during World War I. "Bundles for Britain," "Our Boys Need SOX," "Knit Your Bit," "Knit for Defense," "Remember Pearl Harbor—Purl Harder!" Red Cross posters emblazoned with these slogans brought knitters into the war effort in record numbers. Knitting was the patriotic thing to do once more.

First Lady Eleanor Roosevelt was an enthusiastic knitter. She took her big knit bag everywhere and was often photographed knitting. Big knit bags were all the rage, and knitting in public was a common sight. There was even some controversy about the etiquette of public knitting. It may have been because of the vast number of people doing it. Emily Post, the etiquette maven, advised people not to wave their needles, flap their arms, or pull yarn from their bag with repeated thrusts over their head.[7]

The November 24, 1941, issue of *Life* magazine featured a cover story titled "How to Knit." The article stated, "In answer to the great American question 'What can I do to help the war effort?' the commonest answer yet found is 'Knit.'"[8] When wool became scarce, people picked apart old sweaters and reknit them into usable items.

Many learned how to knit not from a magazine but from Mom or Grandma. And the Red Cross sent out instructors to teach more people. This was a one-on-one, pass-it-along system. Sometimes, though, instruction happened on a much larger scale when a group wanted to learn to knit.

The eight hundred people working in the Butterick Building in New York City decided they wanted to "knit their bit." Few of the mostly women in the building knew how to knit, so they contacted the Red Cross to teach them. In two half-hour lessons, all eight hundred employees learned to knit. The next step was to find out exactly what needed knitting. They contacted the navy and were directed to the Navy League. The league was a little doubtful, but they outlined the knitting needs of two destroyers. In just six weeks—half the time allotted—the Butterick knitters produced a sweater, a pair of gloves, and two pairs of socks for each of the 198 men on board each destroyer. This success inspired them. They requested a new assignment. This time they knit for the crew of the USS *Nevada*, 879 men. The same list of items needed to be knit in just two months. Undaunted, the Butterick knitters set to work and put out an appeal to the one million readers of one of its publications, *The Delineator*. Readers ordered patterns or sent in money to help the cause. Together they met another amazing deadline.[9]

Knitting West to East

Americans were not the only ones knitting their bit. Needs were felt around the world, and knitters filled the need wherever they could.

Soldiers needed knitted items in World War II, but so did thousands of European refugees. Just because the fighting ceased did not mean the need for knitting ended. Anke Betic was a toddler in Germany when World War II broke out, and by the end she was school age. Anke talks about her vivid memories of the war and its aftermath.

"Because of the constant bombing, all the women and children were told to get out of Berlin. Farmers were ordered to take people in. My mother and sister and I went to the country. We stayed in one little room on a farm. It was a lonely situation. The farmer resented us being there. My dad had been drafted into the war. He never shot anyone; however, his work was very dangerous. He drove a gas tanker truck.

"When the war ended, we reunited with my father and returned to the city. Berlin had been divided. We lived in the West with my grandmother for months before we could get a tiny apartment of our own. Travel was restricted in the city. You had to have your papers to go anywhere. If we went to visit the country, we had to cross through two checkpoints in both directions.

"We had so little, and it was very bad. But those in the East had even less. They poured into the West before the border was closed. I remember the Raisin Planes. That's what we called the American Airlift in 1948. Every day for months, planes flew over and dropped supplies. We got tiny bits of dried potatoes, and we'd make a meal out of it. If the Americans hadn't dropped those supplies, I would not be here today. Those planes saved our lives. It was God's provision.

"Thousands of people crossed over from the East. Every day the numbers grew, and refugees filled Berlin. I remember for a few weeks my family had visitors from the East. They would come by train to stay for the day and bring things like their silverware or extra clothes. Some days an envelope of money came through our mail slot. Finally, one day our friends came to visit on the train and they never went back; they stayed in the West. Better to leave for the West with what little you could than to stay in the East.

"Eventually, school started again, and we began knitting at school. We knit twelve-inch squares. I remember it so clearly, knitting square after square. We sewed them together to make blankets for the refugees coming from the East. These people had nothing. Our blankets stayed right in Berlin to help these people. We knit for years. We bought any yarn we could find. We used whatever we had in the house. We found more. We knit and knit. I loved it. We had so little, but we shared what we had. It's what you did."

Anke still knits today. She makes sweaters for her grand-kids, but she also knits for those in need—hats for preemies or scarves for the homeless, even squares for blankets. "I knit lots of squares for Warm Up America!, just like the squares of my childhood. I share what I have. It's God's provision."

Creating History

History is always in the making. We are each a piece of the time line. Our actions and knitting take a place in the estab-lished pattern. Through thousands of people, the craft has made a big impact throughout history. History is personal too. We create a knitted history in our own families. We are the aunt-mom-sister-grandmother who knits. Some churn out many lovely items, and others make a few very special things. Often these items are passed down from generation to generation, creating a history of their own. Ann Gusiff knit a piece of history for her family.

Ann has been knitting for years. She surprised herself when she added it up recently. "I learned to knit when I was seventeen, and with a few short lapses here and there, I've been at it ever since." Her personal knitting history stretches back almost thirty years. She has knit many items for family members over the years: sweaters, scarves, hats, purses, you name it. Ann tells how it began.

"The summer between my junior and senior years of high school, I joined American Field Service and went on a cultural exchange. I loved the independence of it. I went to Aslesund, Norway. It was my first trip abroad. I was just there to soak up the culture. The family I stayed with had a daughter my age who was away on exchange in France. So I was the focus of things that summer. In fact, I ended up in the local paper. Kari, my exchange mom, was a journalist, and she wrote a piece about my coming to town. They took my photo and made a lovely sketch from it, then used it on the front page of the newspaper. I still have the sketch.

"Kari taught me how to knit my first week. In Norway, everyone learned to knit in school. I took to it right away. I had to be shown only a few times, and I just got it. I could pick up a dropped stitch after being shown once. It was very intuitive.

"I like the pattern and texture and repetition of knitting. I've always been into texture and yarn. When I was in first grade, our teacher brought in some needlepoint kits for us. I liked the feel of the yarn in my hands. I liked the repetition of looping it through the holes over and over. I think knitting was just waiting for me with its pattern and repetition.

"My very first sweater that summer in Norway was a traditional Norwegian pattern. I knit a tube straight up and made the sleeves separately. Kari put it together for me. First she used a sewing machine to strengthen the seams. Then it was magic the way she just cut the tube open and inserted the sleeves in place. The sweater is still a favorite.

"Norwegian wool is wonderful. I knit so much that summer in Aslesund that I needed a job to pay for my yarn habit. Since my exchange mom worked at the newspaper, she got me a paper route. I delivered newspapers at five in the morning to big apartment buildings. It was a little crazy, but I wanted to buy a lot of yarn. I came home with the beginnings of my stash and a definite yarn-hoarding habit.

"After college I moved to LA, and my knitting tapered off. It was too hot to knit most of the time. Still, I would drive twenty miles to one of the few knit shops in the area. I loved the textures so much. I'd buy lovely yarns and think of amazing projects to do but did not complete a lot.

"Then my sister announced she was pregnant, and I thought I'd knit something for the new baby. I decided to make a christening gown. I chose a very intricate pattern and used an acrylic blend. I wanted this gown to last. Even though I didn't have children at the time, I envisioned the gown on my own children some day. I wanted it to be a family heirloom.

"It took months of knitting. The pattern was so complicated that I couldn't talk while I knit. It had a seventeen-row repeat. Finally I finished. My niece was in the gown only long enough to take a quick photo. In Southern California, it was too hot for the babe to wear it to the church. But it was the beginning of a tradition. The baptismal gown was passed along to other new babies in our family.

"When we dedicated our first child, the gown came home to me. Each of my three children wore it. Of course, it always seems to be too hot on baptism day, and most of the children had the gown on only long enough for a photo to be taken. Yet it fills my heart to see this tradition in my family. I worry that my daughters will see the gown as a burden. 'Yeah, there's that crazy gown Mom knit when she was young. We *have* to use it.' So I've stored it away with photos of all the babies in our family who have worn it on christening day. I hope my girls will continue to see the tradition as one prompted by love and keep it going."

Mom's Dishcloths

Each knitter is stringing out a personal legacy. There are garments and memories of knitting lessons, but there is also love. When family members and friends remember a knitter, they often think of the love involved in the creation of garments or the patience required in teaching someone to knit.

A knitter's individual history is just as important as the collective history we are all woven into.

Sandie Schuitema shared the story of a lovely knitted legacy.

"My mom was always knitting. She made dishcloths. She knit them constantly. She was active in her church, and when there was a bazaar or fund-raiser, Mom contributed her dishcloths. She also gave them away as gifts.

"I come from a family of five kids. I never thought much about those dishcloths while I was growing up. I didn't see the value in them. After all, not many teens are into washing the dishes. But we always had Mom's knit cloths. When we grew up and moved away, we took dishcloths with us. Mom kept a cupboard full of her boo-boos, those cloths with a mistake in them. So anytime one of us kids went home, we'd raid the cupboard for more dishcloths. We'd take a dozen at a time; she had quite a stockpile. To this day I can't use a store-bought cloth. Mom's were the best.

"In 1998, Mom was diagnosed with urinary tract cancer. This was the same cancer my dad had died from eight years earlier. Mom and all of us kids knew exactly the road she was headed down. She fought the cancer with her doctors and chemo for many months. But by 1999 she was slowing down.

"All five of us kids came home for Christmas that year. Mom was still going to chemo, but we knew it was no longer fighting the cancer as effectively as it had before. One day Mom came home from chemo and was very secretive in her room. We thought she was just tired. Then in the afternoon she came out of her room and called us all together.

"Mom had stopped at the hardware store on the way home and had purchased several dowels about the size of number eight needles. She knew the feel of that size in her hands. She'd cut the dowels into knitting-needle lengths with a hacksaw and then sharpened the ends in a pencil sharpener. She had five sets of needles.

"We all sat down cross-legged on the floor in front of her easy chair. She gave each of us a set of needles and yarn. She also handed out pencils and paper. 'Okay, I'm going to teach you guys how to knit dishcloths.' You know it's funny we never learned to knit as kids. Now ranging in age from thirty-three to fifty-two, we were getting our first lesson. Mom meant business too. She was four foot nine but very stubborn. She wanted to pass along this legacy to us, and we were ready.

"Over that Christmas vacation, each one of us made a dishcloth, even my brother, Kevin. We each wrote down the pattern. For years afterward we all made our own dishcloths. I'm not sure if my siblings are still doing it, but I routinely buy lots of cotton yarn and make dishcloths. I've even started to experiment with colors. I haven't passed the skill along to my kids yet, but there will probably come a time when it's right. For now I knit the dishcloths for my own use and as gifts. I make a dishcloth and crochet a matching potholder and give them away as a set. I have friends who practically cry when they report they have cut a dishcloth with a knife or it's worn out from use. I can be counted on to give them a replacement. I like to give these away at unexpected times too. I usually don't give them for an occasion but rather as an I'm-thinking-of-you gift.

"I'm so glad Mom took the time to show us her dishcloth pattern. It's been a very special way to remember her."

Knitting throughout history has benefited many in need. Sometimes it's the knitter who is in need. The next chapter contains stories about the many benefits knitters receive from the craft. There's more to this knitting business than just a lovely new sweater.

5

At the Same Time

Benefits

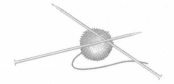

At the same time: used to alert the knitter that more than one change is happening in the pattern simultaneously. Example: shaping the armholes and neck at the same time.

At the same time. If you missed these directions in your pattern, they cause a sinking feeling when you do find them. Probably time to go back and make a correction. Every knitter misses this message at one time or another, but there's good news about "at the same time." While you knit, wonderful things happen. Not only do you finish a lovely sweater for the baby shower or make a terrific pair of socks, but unseen benefits fill your life as well. These are the stirrings you feel at a heart level, things you know in your unconscious self.

And now we have confirmation of the truth. Medical studies prove what we have felt for a long time: knitting is good for you. Knitting offers physical, mental, and spiritual benefits. Among the stories in this chapter, you'll find knitters easing stress, managing chronic pain, and finding a lifelong hobby. So many benefits come to you "at the same time" as you knit. Hooray!

Look What I Found: Time!

Leslie Kamholz has been an everyday knitter for years. It is one of her many passions. Changes were coming though. Another of her passions was about to take over. In the fall of 2009, Leslie started nursing school, an intense pursuit with hours of class work and study. Juggling school and life meant something would have to drop. For Leslie, that something was *not* going to be knitting. Here's how she tells it.

"I'm a very busy person now. I have school every day and a test every week. I also still have to make time for my husband and the cats. When do I have time to knit? I don't. Every moment of my day is planned in advance, leaving me no time for myself. Yet somehow, I knit. I made a decision to make time for knitting. I don't think it really matters what I knit, just that I do. I think when life begins to feel rushed, knitting becomes even more important.

"At the end of the day, my brain turns to mush. So I've been working on a large bag. It's constructed out of rectangles and is all stockinette and seed stitch. I have not done something so wonderfully simple in years. I don't have to think. I don't have to pay attention. I just relax and knit.

"And that's why making time for knitting is so important. Even if you can do it only fifteen minutes a day, do it! It's fifteen minutes when your brain can relax and be creative. It's fifteen minutes just for you. Your brain will thank you for it.

"I'm still learning to make time for sleep, but that's another story."

The Relaxation Response

You know the feeling. You pick up your needles and relax. Your shoulders drop. You take a deep breath and sigh. You probably even have a little smile on your face. A tune may pop in your head. Leslie Kamholz described how knitting during nursing school helped to manage stress levels. It turns out that other people have studied this knitting phenomenon scientifically, and it is very real.

For over twenty-five years at the Benson-Henry Institute for Mind Body Medicine, researchers have studied the connection between stress and physical health. (The Benson-Henry Institute is connected to the Harvard School of Medicine at Massachusetts General Hospital.) Dr. Benson and his colleagues have noted that you can put the body in a meditative state with a variety of techniques such as repetitive prayer, tai chi, yoga, jogging, and, yes, knitting. They call it the relaxation response. It's the pleasant alternative to a fight-or-flight response. Instead of your heart racing with fear, your heart rate can actually lower eleven beats a minute. Ah, the relaxation response.[1]

There are only two steps necessary for eliciting the relaxation response. First, use a repetitive word, sound, phrase, prayer, or muscular movement (such as knitting). Second, passively disregard everyday thoughts that inevitably come to mind and return to your repetition. Within just ten to twenty minutes, you can feel the relaxation response. (Though if you can stop knitting after just ten minutes, I'm impressed. I always want to finish the next pattern repeat!)

The Benson-Henry website notes, "Regular elicitation of the relaxation response has been scientifically proven to be an effective treatment for a wide range of stress-related disorders. In fact, to the extent that any disease is caused or made worse by stress, the relaxation response can help."[2] See, you knew it all along. Knitting is good for you.

Stitchlinks

Stitchlinks.com is a support network for those who use knitting and stitching therapeutically. It offers articles on topics such as explaining pain, talking to your doctor, and heart facts. There appears to be a knowledge gap between what goes on in research and what the typical patient knows, so the site tries to close the gap. The Stitchlinks forum provides a safe place for people to talk openly and is successful in helping people build social confidence. Of course, there's a story behind the site.

In 2002 Betsan Corkhill was working as a senior physiotherapist. Many of her patients had long-term medical conditions such as chronic pain, depression, or neurological problems that often isolated them. Most had lost interest and motivation, so it was difficult for them to do the exercises Betsan left or carry out the advice she gave. She felt they needed to develop an interest in the world again before they could adhere to a program of physical therapy. Betsan became frustrated with a system that didn't cater to the whole person—body, mind, and spirit—and decided on a major career change.

Betsan became a freelance production editor for a range of magazines. One day she was asked to work on a craft portfolio and discovered a treasure trove of anecdotal evidence on the therapeutic benefits of knitting and stitching. "I immediately thought of my patients, so I decided it warranted further investigation. I began to think of ways I could get the message across to others who might benefit. Naturally, a website came to mind. Stitchlinks was born in January 2005."

Betsan talks further about Stitchlinks and current research.

"My initial thoughts were that knitting and stitching could provide an easily accessible way of occupying those who were housebound. It's been known for some time that occupied people feel less pain and depression than those who do nothing. It was clear from the anecdotal evidence that knitting and stitching were powerful distractions, enabling people to literally take their mind off even severe pain. However, as I continued to dig, it became clear that the benefits were much deeper than simply distraction. These knitters and stitchers experienced changed attitudes and became motivated to do other activities.

"Stitchlinks is a site where people can share their story as well as find out more information about the connections between knitting and health. The narratives we've received bear out my feelings that the issues of social isolation, low self-esteem, fear, anxiety, and worry need to be dealt with alongside medical issues. It's my experience that no matter how excellent the medical treatment, if these issues are left unaddressed, the patient will continue to have significant problems. Quality of life matters. Healthy people should also pay heed to these issues as a preventative measure.

"Knitting and stitching are effective in dealing with these issues and are ideal complements to medical treatments. Together with experts in pain management and depression, psychologists, and health care workers, we've formed a number of theories we aim to test with controlled research. Just imagine doctors prescribing a dose of stitching twice a day. Impossible? Doctors and nurses already refer patients to a group I run at a local hospital. Stitching and knitting cannot cure our ills; however, researching how these activities can help manage symptoms is a worthwhile pursuit.

"I think, through our research, knitting and stitching could form the basis of significant therapies in the not-too-distant future. We have several studies looking for funding. One study looks at the effect of knitting on memory span and recall. It is based at Cardiff University, Wales, UK. A second proposed study explores the effect of knitting on the experience of chronic pain. This one is based at the Pain Management Unit of the Royal United Hospital in Bath, UK. Research is happening, and we will be a part of it.

"I also have a new knitting site: iknitlinks.org. This site was born out of my friendship with Gerard at I Knit London. We want to make a difference in the world through knitting. Our mission is to set up a network of knitting groups with the purpose of building local communities and providing an infrastructure for the local groups to communicate globally. Our aim is to have groups of knitters from all backgrounds, beliefs, and age groups mixing and making friends. Our hope is that the individuals will grow in self-esteem and social confidence through learning a new skill and sharing their knitting. Iknitlinks also gives us another way to spread the knowledge about the benefits of knitting to your health."

Betsan Corkhill follows her own best advice and research. She uses knitting to manage her stress levels and tries to do a little every evening. "It helps me to sleep when lots of ideas are whirring around in my head!" And this is a woman with lots of good ideas to manage.

"Are You Okay?"

"I've heard knitting helps you manage stress. Can you teach me how to knit?" Marci Seither asked her sister-in-law to show her the basics. Marci's firstborn, Nathan, had just joined the Marines. Nathan's decision not only changed his life path but also affected his entire family. Marci discovered that knitting calmed her heart in ways she never expected. Here's her story.

"I wasn't surprised by Nathan's decision to enter the military. While most little kids idolized Superman or the Hulk, Nathan's hero was Columbo. He was the only one in his third-grade class who owned his own trench coat and message decoder. When the Twin Towers crumbled and our country was mourning, I asked Nathan how he felt about his lifelong dream of being in the FBI.

"Without hesitation he responded, 'Mom, they need good guys in there.' He was right. I just didn't think the day would come so soon.

"After graduating from high school, Nathan made an announcement. He'd researched several options and had decided to pursue the Marine Corp Security Forces. The next afternoon he would be reporting to the local recruiter's office to start the paperwork. My heart stopped. I was not ready to jump into this new phase of parenting. We have six children and have done a lot of parenting, but this was new territory. I thought of all the reasons Nathan was not ready to leave home, but in my heart I knew he was ready to go. It was time for him to live his own life to the fullest. Still, I ended up in my bedroom behind a locked door sobbing into my pillow.

"I took up knitting the minute Nathan made his announcement. Weeks before he left for boot camp, I had already produced numerous scarves.

"Nathan wasn't the only family member bringing change to our household. The beginning of 2005 was rough. At the end of January, our eldest daughter, Emma, graduated early from high school and then fulfilled a dream to be a foreign exchange student. She left to live with my husband's brother and his family in Saipan for six months. Then in March, Nathan shipped off to boot camp. And on April 1, my dear cousin Jeff died of leukemia. Jeff was my age. We'd grown up together. I had been tested in hopes of being a bone marrow donor, but despite my pleadings with the Lord, I wasn't a match. Those first months of 2005 felt almost unbearable. Thank heaven for Christ and knitting. I knew when Nathan decided to go into the Marines I would need something to help me get through. I knew knitting was good for stress relief, but I never dreamed what saving grace knitting would bring in 2005.

"I bought ten skeins of yarn to get started. I am a color and tactile person. I also like to see progress. So I worked with bulky yarn and big needles. The process was the most important part for me in the beginning. It was so stressful when Nathan left that I knit all the time. I held on so tightly that I even bent my needles. Sometimes my husband would call on his way home from work, and I'd ask him to pick up more yarn.

"'What kind do you want?' he'd ask.

"'Anything.'

"'Having a bad day?'

"'I need to keep knitting. Surprise me with any yarn you can find.'

"Knitting saved my sanity. I could slow down the thoughts racing through my head. It's like when you are driving in the car. If you rush by at 60 miles per hour, you see very little of what's going on around you. But if you slow down and walk, you can see a butterfly floating or flowers growing. That's what knitting does for me. It slows me down so I can process and see what is important. I can rest in the knowledge that God is in control.

"Knitting became a discipline of prayer for me. I knit scarves for everyone I knew. I took great care to pick out the right yarn for each person. Then as I knit I thought of the person getting the scarf. I held them in prayer. It's very calming to concentrate on a loved one and knit for them. I made so many scarves that everyone got a handmade gift for Christmas. It was a hug from me to them. I ended up with lots of little leftovers. I took all those extra tidbits and knit them into a scarf for myself. Now when I wear it, I look at the different colors and remember each person represented. This is yet another way to stay close to my family and friends and hold them in prayer. And it makes me smile.

"Nathan's leaving affected our entire family. His brothers and sisters missed him just as much as I did. I was not the only one worried about Nathan. My youngest son, Jack, was a first grader when Nathan left. At the beginning of the school year, Jack was an accomplished reader. By Christmas he was a struggling nonreader. His teacher was concerned, and we brainstormed ways to help him. I didn't need to think long. I told her to give me the curriculum. I would teach him at home. He was so stressed that he couldn't function in a classroom. So Jack and I did 'full contact phonics.' He needed to touch family, to physically lean into me and know I was there with him. We dealt with our worries together as best we could. He saw I had found knitting to deal with my stress, and so we found a way for him to deal with his. In several months, Jack was reading again and ready to go back to the classroom.

"I feel it's really important to model healthy habits for my kids. And dealing with stress is a habit they need to acquire. I love the quote from Dr. Howard Hendricks: 'You cannot impart what you do not possess.' I needed an outlet for my stress. And after what we went through with Jack, I realized how important it was for my kids to find ways of dealing with their stress too. We acknowledged that we were all concerned about Nathan and the changes in our family. Knitting made me a better mom.

"Just before Thanksgiving in 2009, a black Jeep Cherokee pulled into our driveway. Nathan stepped out and wrapped me in a powerful embrace. He was home—not on a long pass or a leave after deployment. He was home for good. His five years of service were complete.

"'Well, Mom,' he said, 'this is the end of an era.'

"I was giddy with excitement. It was the end of an era for me as well. As the mother of a Marine, I had sent countless care packages filled with homemade cookies and warm socks. All the while, I wondered if I would have the strength and courage to handle the news delivered by a military chaplain should the unthinkable happen.

"As I looked at Nathan, I thought of an Old Testament verse: 'There is a time for everything, a season for every purpose under heaven . . . a time to weep and a time to laugh, a time to mourn and a time to dance.'

"I hugged Nathan again. All the fears I had had while he was patrolling the desert of Afghanistan melted away. For now, the season of weeping and worrying was over. Nathan was home, and it was time to laugh.

"Motherhood is full of surprises—some good, some difficult. There are moments you wish you could capture in a jar in order to savor them later. There are also times when it feels like you're being dragged through a bitter cold Minnesota winter. One of the things I learned during Nathan's time in the Marines was that laughter and dancing are even sweeter after all the weeping and mourning are over. While I am thankful Nathan is home once again, his return is sweeter because of his prolonged absence.

"Knitting continues at my house. My husband, John, still gets a little nervous when he comes home and hears my needles clicking. 'Are you okay?' he asks. These days I can say, 'Yes, I am fine.' Knitting is still my solace of choice when I am under stress, but it's also my relaxation when I just want to unwind after a busy day. It slows my pace, and I settle into thoughts and prayers for loved ones. With everything going on, knitting is something I can do that keeps me from becoming unraveled."

Staff Sergeant Sorich Knits

Military knitting calls to mind the millions of items knit for soldiers serving our country. But some of those soldiers are knitters too. Staff Sergeant John Sorich IV was deployed to Iraq in January 2009, and before shipping out he tossed his knitting into his duffle. John's knitting was not a newfound interest. He'd been at it for a while.

"When I was in high school, I got interested in World War II. I used to watch the History Channel all the time. Fort Snelling is on the river in Minnesota, near my home. I was at an event there one Memorial Day weekend and saw some historical reenactors. I had no idea what they were all about, but I was intrigued. I started talking to them about their group. I ended up getting more and more information and eventually joined the Minnesota Historical Re-Enactors Society.

"After high school, I attended Minnesota State and got my degree in corrections. I went to work at the Hennepin County Home School. This is a place for juvenile offenders ages thirteen to seventeen. And just about everyone there knits, from the staff to the residents. They found that knitting helps settle the kids. It gives them a focus and a feeling of accomplishment. They have pride in their work when they finish a piece. And the knitting counts toward their required community service hours. When I joined the staff, Sandra Yang taught me to knit. I'd already been a crocheter. When I was in high school and snowboarding all the time, it was hip to crochet your own caps. All kinds of guys were doing it.

"I stayed active in the historical reenactors and was always on the lookout for more authentic items to add to my uniform. I've made some items. For example, I built my own munitions box when I couldn't find an authentic replica. My knitting fed into this too. I wanted to have a hat accurate for the time period and couldn't find one, so I decided to knit one of my own. I found a pattern from 1943, a watch cap.

"My first attempt took quite a while, but now I can make a cap without even making a hash mark on a piece of paper. I've got the pattern memorized. I matched the color of yarn to an original US World War II glove that was knit by the Red Cross. It's Cascade Yarns 220 Heathers color #9459, an olive army color. It's great yarn to work with and the closest color I have found to the original. I think it is about the same size and weight of what was used in the 1940s.

"In Iraq, the regular 120-degree heat and daily work were enough to drive a person insane. Knitting was not the first thought on my mind. But when the weather started to cool, I pulled out my knitting. In October, a fellow sergeant in my platoon asked about my cap. He thought it was cool. I told him I made it. That surprised him; it's such a tight knit. 'Could you teach me how to do that?' I didn't expect that kind of enthusiasm. Word got around, and our knitting group was born.

"At first a lot of the guys thought it was weird. 'You're knitting?' No one could understand why I wanted to do it. 'This is weird? You play World of Warcraft all day.'

"But after they saw what we were making, they were really supportive and wanted to see the finished pieces. People started asking if we were going to knit in the evening, and the group grew. We had ten guys knitting regularly.

"Knitting wasn't just a productive thing for us to do; it gave everyone involved a different skill to be proud of. As people finished their projects, they proudly brought them around to other knitters and non-knitters and showed off their work. It did more than you think; it was a great stress reliever!

"Knitting offered an easy way to concentrate on something other than our mundane work. The routine can be very dull. But then getting ready for a mission would be very stressful. There could be many different endings to a mission. Someone could be killed or wounded, or vehicles could break down. There were a lot of unknowns. Knitting kept our minds on something new and different.

"The 1940s watch cap was the most popular thing to make, wear, and give away. It is not army regulation anymore, but it is nice to wear in your civilian life. Then around November, our group went into full-scale production making scarves and hats. Many made items for their kids or their spouse in time for Christmas. I think it was the perfect way to show our families that they're still in our thoughts, even though we're far away. I now have a great deal of respect and pride for the mothers, grandmothers, children, and men who knit during the wars for the fighting military men. It is amazing to think of an entire nation of knitters all striving to outfit the millions of troops in the US armed forces during such dire times.

"I came home from Iraq with ten knit caps I made for my friends, two wristlets, and the spiral-patterned sock—all total about seventy-four thousand stitches. I'm an engineer; we count things. My sister Naomi had sent care packages of yarn to our group while I was deployed. She made regular trips to Needlework Unlimited in Minneapolis. When I got home, I made a stop in the shop to thank them and let them see what I'd made out of the yarn. They were so enthusiastic. It was fun to share my knitting with them."

John is still knitting, of course. After his stop at Needlework Unlimited, he took off for a vacation to New Zealand, where there are four million people and twelve million sheep. "There is a lot of wool. Everyone seems to knit or be connected to the wool industry in some way. I went by so many knit shops. I came home with a lot of wool. I'd see a particular color and know just the person I wanted to knit a hat for. My mom is a knitter too, and so I brought home some yarn for her." John is keeping it in the family, the big family of knitters, and enjoying the many benefits of the craft, from stress release to the pleasure of giving away a finished product.

The Learning Curve

Sitting around the Tuesday knit circle, I watched scarves and hats grow on the needles of the group. Each person carefully placed the next stitch. Their calm faces seemed to indicate they enjoyed what they were doing. But many of these people were beginners and had been knitting only a few weeks or months. How did they acquire such easy confidence?

Kate, crafting her first scarf ever, said it took a while to get the hang of knitting. "When I started, it was as if I had never used my hands before."

I nodded. I remembered that frustrated feeling in the beginning, but I couldn't remember what drove me to continue. I asked the group, "Why did you stick with it?"

Kate explained, "I saw other people knitting, and their hands were filled with such grace. I wanted that."

Beth piped in, "It's just two sticks and some yarn. How hard can it be? I had to master it."

Mike, who had learned to knit a month before, said, "Well, Beth got me started. I walked by one Tuesday and they were having fun, so I tried it. I was looking for a hobby that had nothing to do with the glow of a screen." Several others in the group nodded in agreement. This work group all sat before glowing screens every day. Feeling work in their hands was a satisfying switch.

Though the benefits of knitting sometimes seem hidden, they are visible enough for the novice to want to learn to knit. But to reap the rewards, you have to climb the learning curve. Some discover this just isn't their thing, and they never make it over the first rise of frustration. But for those who really take to it, patience and persistence allow them to soar and reap the benefits.

Lifelong Knitter

Knitters seem to pick up and put down the craft over a lifetime. Those of us fond of playing with yarn and needles know the value of what we've got. There is no need to spell out the benefits for us. We feel it. Just let us knit. I found a knitter who's been well aware of the benefits for many, many years.

Lloyd Harvey is a champion swimmer and baseball pitcher, unpublished novelist, and lifelong knitter. At "lifelong" we'd better pause for a moment: Lloyd turned 106 on September 2, 2010. He was born in 1904 in Republican City,

Nebraska. This is a man who does not take any medications, lives in his own home, navigates the twenty-six stairs in the house all day long, and has a bowl of ice cream each evening. Please don't forget the Snickers bar to go with that!

There were twelve children in the Harvey family. Lloyd is the third oldest. When he was growing up in the farm country of Nebraska, his grandmother needed looking after. She was sick and prone to spells. All the other kids would disappear when asked to sit with Grandma. Lloyd didn't mind the task, though. He spent many days caring for her. He'd walk into town to get her medicines and groceries, then out to her farm to look after her. Of course, there was no radio or television to entertain them, so one afternoon Grandma decided to teach Lloyd to knit. He took to it. He knit with his grandma most days after that. He never took his knitting home or let others know he'd learned how to use yarn and needles. He was a ten-year-old boy after all.

The one time Lloyd's health betrayed him he was thirty. Sitting on the front porch reading the paper, Lloyd had some chest pains. The doctor came; in those days there were house calls. The doctor put Lloyd to bed immediately. "You're having a heart attack." Not too long after the doc left, Lloyd was back on the porch reading the paper. He hadn't finished yet. That heart attack kept Lloyd out of the military. He couldn't sign up and was disappointed about it, but he found another way to contribute to the war effort.

This was the time of the Red Cross Knit Your Bit campaign. Lloyd's wife, Freda, went to help out at the local Red Cross in Norton, Kansas. Freda did fine embroidery and crochet but as a left-hander couldn't quite get the hang of knitting. She brought home piles of yarn and tried hard. Finally, Lloyd asked if he could take a look. Freda showed him what she was supposed to make, and in no time he'd knit all the yarn into the items the Red Cross needed. Lloyd was still shy about his knitting, and so they sent back all the work under the guise that Freda had completed it.

Knitting was not man's work—yet. If anyone came over to the house, Lloyd quickly hid his needles under a seat cushion. Freda was under strict orders not to talk about it to anyone. Finally, one summer Freda was helping process all the entries for the Norton County Fair and secretly entered one of Lloyd's afghans using his own name. He won grand champion! His response was, "It's a joke, right? You're kidding me, aren't you, Freda?" It was the truth, and there was an angry neighbor to prove it. Seems the grand champion in town was usually the same woman and was none too pleased to be bumped from her spot by a man. After this Lloyd wasn't so shy about his knitting. He let Freda enter whatever she wanted each year in the fair. He was grand champion many times over.

Lloyd and Freda both came from large families. Lloyd was one of twelve, and Freda was one of eight. They decided, though, to have only one child. But their daughter, Marlene, had lots of cousins. Aunt Freda and Uncle Lloyd always made sure each cousin had an individual gift under the tree at Christmastime. Some years that was the only gift they got. One year Lloyd wrote to all the mothers asking them to trace each child's hand. He made a pair of gloves for each niece and nephew. Marlene got a pair too. She still has them and admires the craftsmanship. Lloyd taught his daughter to knit and purl; however, Marlene is the first to tell you that's the extent of her knowledge. "I can make a dishcloth, but Dad's work is beautiful. Never a dropped stitch anywhere."

Lloyd's knitting fame grew in Norton, Kansas. The doctor in town, who had a very large house, asked Lloyd to knit an afghan for each room. Lloyd took the job. He went to look at the colors in each room, made his yarn selections, and then created something different for each room. Keep in mind that Lloyd was also raising his own family and working full-time as foreman at the Johnson Fruit Company.

Lloyd still knits every day. He makes dishcloths. The rugs and afghans are too big these days. An antique dealer in a town nearby carries his wares, and they sell quite well. In the autumn, Lloyd starts stocking up. Folks in town know they can stop by and make a holiday purchase. Lloyd's dishcloths make great stocking stuffers. He loves the visitors too. You get so much more than a little holiday gift when you purchase one of Lloyd's creations.

All these sales feed Lloyd's knitting habit. He buys more yarn to keep things going. Lloyd loves life and every day asks Marlene, "Where are we going to go today?" That is, "Where are we going after I finish this row?"

The unseen benefits of knitting warm our hearts. We feel the need to knit and come to find out the feeling eases us in a physical way. Now let's look outward and find others who need the benefits of our knitting. The next chapter is about people who need the items we produce.

6

Pick Up Stitches

Charities

Pick up stitches: to create a new row of live stitches at the edge of a row of established knitting.

It's the nature of this craft to give it away. Few knitters can wear all they produce. Giving something hand-knit to an unsuspecting recipient is a thrill. Many knitters have an organization they are passionate about and knit for all year long. There are so many worthy causes; sometimes it's impossible to choose. Yet I have found there is usually a group that touches a person's heart, and they pour their efforts into that cause. Maybe you have a son or daughter in the military, and knitting for our troops appeals to you. Or you knit a prayer shawl for a loved one and found such benefit that you wanted to make shawls for others as well. Possibly knitting for children is a passion, so a children's charity gets all your attention.

If you've not tried knitting for an organization, maybe it's time for you to pick up some stitches for charity. Choices of charity projects range from head to toe. I've collected a few to highlight. A search on the web will show you many more to choose from. The story behind the charity is often quite interesting. It is no surprise to learn that many of them started as tiny grassroots efforts and grew to national, even international, proportions with thousands of knitters participating. I certainly hope you find an outlet here for the love waiting to flow from your needles.

Guideposts Knit for Kids

In 1996, Bridgette Weeks wrote a *Guideposts* article about knitting for refugees. She remembered from her childhood the fulfilling feeling of knitting for others. She ended her article with an invitation for readers to join her. Knitters responded, and many requested the pattern mentioned in the article. Sweaters started pouring into the *Guideposts* offices. This was not a passing fancy; readers kept sending their gifts of love. Since those simple beginnings, half a million sweaters have arrived. *Guideposts* devoted a group to managing the project and operated as a distribution center.

Guideposts Knit for Kids got me knitting again after a decade of idle needles. I've read *Guideposts* magazine for years. I'm a big fan. When I saw the article highlighting their Knit for Kids program, it got me wondering. *Do I even remember how to cast on? Could I work this simple pattern?* I reread the article and got excited. My mom refreshed my memory for casting on, and I was off.

Over the years, *Guideposts* has worked with several charitable organizations in distributing the sweaters. World Vision was a key partner. World Vision is a Christian humanitarian organization dedicated to helping children, their families, and communities worldwide to overcome poverty and injustice. Looking to increase the impact of this strong ministry, *Guideposts* decided to turn the program over to World Vision. In 2009, World Vision became the new clearinghouse for the Knit for Kids Program. Their reach is global. In the past ten years, they have helped *Guideposts* bring knitted gifts to children as far away as Azerbaijan, Kenya, and Thailand, and as close as West Virginia, New Orleans, and the Bronx. *Guideposts* is still connected to the project, but World Vision handles the day-to-day operations.

Knit for Kids offers one simple pattern. It's easy enough for a beginner to complete with pride and offers the accomplished knitter a canvas to embellish with color and stitch patterns. There's also an aran pattern to challenge the more advanced knitter, as well as a crochet pattern. One pattern is used so that when the boxes of sweaters are opened, the only decision is, "Which color do I want?" There aren't vast differences in sweater design and construction. The intention is to delight, not to cause bickering and hurt feelings.

I love to knit for *Guideposts*. It is my charity of choice. It's fun to try out new stitches and color patterns. I have several ways to enhance the simple design. I select several colors for a sweater and then use a different stitch pattern for each color change. Or I practice color work by knitting in an intarsia picture or geometric blocks of color. And this simple sweater design also gives me an excuse to buy wild variegated yarns and watch them change color on my needles. I know all these variations will delight a child somewhere.

If you would like to get involved with the Knit for Kids program, here is the website: www.knitforkids.org. You will find free downloadable patterns, you can read more about their current needs, and you can see pictures and read stories of how the sweaters are received. Their mailing address is Knit for Kids, World Vision, 210 Overlook Drive, Sewickley, PA 15143.

Warm Up America!

Warm Up America! (WUA) is a very popular knitting charity. Thousands of people from church groups to school kids have knit squares for WUA. Like all good ideas, it started small and took root.

In 1991, Evie Rosen owned the Knitting Nook in Wausau, Wisconsin. She had two concerns. First, she wanted to do something for the homeless. Second, she, like every other knitter, had accumulated quite a collection of stray balls of yarn. A perfect pairing was born. She decided to knit the remnants into squares and sew the squares into cozy afghans. Evie soon had customers, friends, and family knitting and crocheting afghans galore. She received national attention from articles in the *Milwaukee Journal Sentinel* and *Crafts* magazine. In fact, things went so well that in 1994 Evie turned to the Craft Yarn Council of America for help. This is a nonprofit association of yarn companies and publishers, and today they run Warm Up America!, though Evie continues to be involved.

Here's how WUA works. Local groups such as church organizations, classrooms of school children, or neighbors come together and volunteer to knit or crochet rectangles that are 7 x 9 inches. These are then sewn together into finished blankets measuring 49 x 63 inches. Then the blankets are donated to those in need through local charities: women's shelters, nursing homes, day care centers, and hospices—anyone who needs to be wrapped in a little love. If you are not involved with a local group, you can still make squares and send them to the WUA foundation, where volunteers sew the squares together into blankets and then distribute them.

Warm Up America! is far more than a stash buster. It's a community builder. The very idea of WUA is to have neighbors help neighbors. Keeping the blankets local is an important part of WUA, and participants are encouraged to work in groups to make afghans. To get involved, check out their website at www.craftyarncouncil.com/warmup.html.

Head Huggers

When the Twin Towers fell on September 11, 2001, the effects of the disaster rippled throughout the world. Thousands of people across the country felt the need to do something. Sue Thompson was a knitter with a unique response.

"I developed an incredible need to do something nice for this world, preferably in some small, quiet way. I wasn't sure what form this would take. Then in October I met Pam Mitchell, a dear friend of my sister-in-law. Pam was going through chemotherapy for breast cancer. I asked her if she experienced any side effects. Her only complaint was a cold head from losing her hair. Thinking of Pam on my way home and knowing I love to knit, I decided to make her a few soft caps. As I knit Pam's caps, it occurred to me that a lot of people out there experienced chemotherapy and probably also had cold heads. That's when the idea to start Head Huggers began.

"At first I was overwhelmed by the idea. Who was I to think I could pull this off? But then I realized that if I didn't do it, it might not get done. Head Huggers was all up to me. While it's a lot of work, all the decisions are mine. I made a to-do list and soon discovered that tackling things one at a time resulted in rapid success. I've learned a lot throughout this entire process. Sometimes I even surprise my husband with my newfound computer expertise.

"I believe a higher power was at work from the beginning because things fell into place so easily for me. Being retired and on a fixed income, I was eager to keep my expenses down. But contributions came my way one after another. First, my nephew, who has a master's degree in computer science and had already created several outstanding websites for others, agreed to do mine for free.

"Next, a good friend agreed to help me write the pages I needed for the website. I wrote and she critiqued. But she was so good at writing that she ended up rewriting many of the pages for me.

"Then I asked another good friend, a very creative retired high school art teacher, if she would design a logo for me. She too was gracious and fulfilled my request for free. She did a wonderful job.

"Next, I needed knitting supplies. Of course, price was still an issue. I started telling anyone and everyone about my project. Friends who go to garage sales started looking for yarn. When they told the sellers what the goods were being used for, they often received the yarn for free. Also, I wrote to several large yarn companies, sending them my brochure and asking them to check my website to verify my project. Coats and Clark Yarn Company responded with a box so large that my husband and I could barely lift it! In fact, they continue to send me large boxes filled with yarn whenever I make a request. That was only the beginning. Lion Brand Yarn Company also sent a large box of really soft yarns. More recently, Bernat Yarn Company sent a large shipment of great yarn.

"The word continues to spread, and hats flood my home. I am very busy now with collecting, labeling, and dispensing chemo caps. Since I began in December of 2001, I've personally distributed over sixty thousand hats. I keep a record of where and how many caps I send to each cancer site. I also send thank you notes to each volunteer who knits for me.

"The hats go all over the country. I searched the internet and found a listing for the Associations of Community Cancer Centers, which lists hundreds of centers by state. From there I get addresses of places to send the hats. In addition, I send hats to oncologists' offices, often because a request came to me from one of the patients. Sometimes I get requests from oncology nurses.

"Of course, all this time I knit. I made the first forty to fifty hats myself. There are hundreds of knitters and crocheters involved now. A group of ninety-year-old ladies at a nearby assisted living residence makes forty to sixty caps for me each month. One of them has crocheted over two hundred caps in the past year and a half. I pick them up monthly and occasionally even join their knitting circle.

"Hats arrive from across the country. I found if I splintered off a group, knitters could fill the need for hats in their area. This is why I developed the idea of satellite groups to keep things local and help defray my expenses. Now I have ninety groups in thirty-two states. We've even gone international with groups in Australia, Canada, Germany, Puerto Rico, and the UK. It is easier for the really active knitters to use my brochures and give caps locally rather than sending them to me for distribution. Everyone is more productive this way. The hats are free of charge, though at my husband's request, I have a gently worded request for donations on my website.

"I keep track of my satellite groups. Once a year I check in with every one to see if they are still active or if I need to remove them from the list on the website. It's a lot of work, but I enjoy it. In fact, I have been having so much fun that I've started a new charity–knitting and sewing for newborns, clients of crisis pregnancy centers, and maternity homes. You'll have to check out my new website: www.miracleshappen.us."

Sue's enthusiasm knows no bounds. She is very active with her charity work. If you'd like to join Head Huggers, you can find Sue online at www.headhuggers.org. There you can look for a group in your area or find out how to launch a new satellite group. The site provides guidelines for getting started, whether you want to knit a few hats to send in or start a group of your own. Patterns and brochures are ready to go, and they're all free. Chilly heads are waiting for a hug from you.

Operation Toasty Toes

Irene Silliman has been knitting for nearly seventy years and is famous among family and friends for her slippers. If you own a pair, treasure them. These days you have to wait in a long line to get a set. Irene's first priority is the military. Even family members beg for a pair, but their requests go unanswered for now because Operation Toasty Toes comes first.

In February of 1997, Bob Silliman, Irene's husband, lost his two-year battle with cancer. Irene put on a brave face. She didn't want her family to think she was suffering; she wanted to stay strong for them. But as her first Christmas alone approached, Irene got blue. Then a letter arrived from her grandson. David Ward was a navy cryptologist stationed on the USS *Carney* in the Persian Gulf. Like any good grandson, David thanked his grandmother for the delicious brownies she'd sent. He also wondered if she could make him (and a few of his buddies) a pair of her famous slippers, "just like Granddad's." What perfect timing. Of course Irene could make a few pairs of her special slippers. She started knitting.

Irene's slippers had served in the military before. Her husband, Bob, had a pair with him while he was a POW for two years in Korea. With the help of two friends, Irene sent David and his shipmates one hundred pairs of slippers for the winter. When the box dropped on deck via helicopter, the officer in charge puzzled over the label: *Operation Toasty Toes?* He only wondered a moment. Then he saw a young sailor rushing toward him jumping up and down and yelling, "They're here! The booties are here!" David snagged the first pair, and the other ninety-nine were gone in no time.

"Nothing like this has boosted morale in a long time," the grateful grandson wrote his grandma. Could she please make 220 more pairs for the rest of the crew on board? Of course. Irene swung into action, enlisting the aid of a growing army of volunteers. Operation Toasty Toes really took off.

Irene is quick to tell you, "God blessed this from the beginning. He took an old lady and gave her a mission." Once David's crew all had slippers, Irene just kept knitting. David's wife, Julie, was stationed on another ship, and Irene decided to knit a pair of slippers for everyone on board her vessel as well. Of course, Irene didn't realize aircraft carriers have a crew of 5,500. No matter. Irene and her volunteers went to work, and soon all those on the aircraft carrier sported Toasty Toes as well.

Getting the slippers to the right location is no mean feat. Packages must be addressed to a specific soldier or sailor. This makes each package's destination a moving target. Irene enlisted the help of her congressman Steve LaTourette. Not only did her slippers find the right drop zone but Congressman LaTourette even reimbursed her for the cost of that first package. This helped Operation Toasty Toes get rolling. LaTourette went a step further in the following years. When the congressman took a trip to Iraq, he hand delivered two hundred pairs of slippers. The Toasty Toes organization is run exclusively on donations. Yarn, boxes, and labels all are paid for through donations. And this has been sustained since 1997.

Each pair of slippers gets tagged with the Operation Toasty Toes logo and a note of encouragement from the knitter, with name and address. The notes are very important. Knitters want the servicemen and -women to know that a real person cares for them personally. The operation's logo is a drawing of Rusty, Irene's dog. The logo shows Rusty with a pair of slippers in his mouth waiting for his master to return. Many letters of thanks come back to the knitters. Irene saves each one she receives. Whenever she gets weary, she reads a few. From sergeant to admiral and seaman to chaplain, they are all grateful.

"The bright colors made us laugh."

"It's wonderful to know the people back home haven't forgotten us and appreciate the sacrifices we make to serve our country."

"I wish I could share with you all the smiles and high spirits that are running through my squadron at this moment."

"For some soldiers this is the only Christmas gift they will get this year."

And this excerpt from a 2006 letter from Rear Admiral Mark Buzby: "I have taken them [slippers] to sea with me to keep my feet comfortable since 1997. They are now a part of my sea bag for the rest of my career. On behalf of the thousands of sailors that you and your Toasty Toes ladies have touched over the years with your gift of slippers and words of support, I offer you my most sincere and loving thanks for just being there for us. It means more to us than you can ever imagine. God bless you, and a big Navy hug from us all!"

The admiral was not the only one to recognize what a contribution Irene and Toasty Toes make to the military. Awards and recognition pour over Irene. Many have honored her. In 2004, the Operation Desert Shield Desert Storm Association awarded Irene the National Patriot Award. She was reluctant to accept because while she knows she was the catalyst, she acknowledges that she is not the only person knitting. Always reluctant to take accolades, Irene was persuaded to accept the honor on behalf of all the volunteers who knit. And that is quite a large number of volunteers. In 2004, when Irene accepted her award, Operation Toasty Toes had produced well over fifty thousand slippers. The number continues to grow.

Operation Toasty Toes currently has twenty-one chapters all over the United States and now one in Canada. Toasty Toes gives people at home a way to honor the sacrifices the fighting men and women make on their behalf. Civilians reach out and care for the military. During World War I and II, knitters rallied to make socks. Unfortunately, the war to end all wars did not end all conflict, and needs continue. Many who have not knitted in years find their dusty needles and unused skeins of yarn and put them to good use. Knitting offers a way to encourage both the citizen and the soldier. And Operation Toasty Toes needs all the knitters it can muster.

If you want to let someone in the armed services know you appreciate their sacrifice, join Operation Toasty Toes. There is probably a chapter near you. Their website is www .operationtoastytoes.org. Or you can contact Irene Silliman at 5232 North Ridge Road, Madison, OH 44057. She still sends boxes from her home. In fact, Irene jokes that her attic is a yarn warehouse. Now in her eighties, Irene continues to knit every day for the project so dear to her heart because the waiting list for slippers continues to grow. Irene marvels, "And to think it all started in my kitchen. I always tell people God works in mysterious ways."

Send Money

The outpouring of knitted garments sent around the world is huge. Fund-raising and volunteerism keep charities going. Bente Petersen, owner of Piedmont Yarn and Apparel in Oakland, California, takes a different view of knitting for charity. Bente firmly believes in the charity work; however, she feels the knitting should stay home while the money goes out.

Bente explains her point of view.

"We have to take into consideration what we are sending. Our charity work should provide the most good possible. I have two examples of work I see going on that may be done with the best of intentions but I feel is not suited for the recipients.

"First, there are many people knitting teddy bears and sending them to Africa. It's a lovely thought, but those children have no reference to teddy bears. A toy lion or giraffe maybe, but not bears. And the amount of money and effort it takes to get those toys where they are going is roughly the amount of money needed to keep a child in school for a year. My uncle used to send two hundred dollars a year to a family he sponsored in Mali. Eight children were able to go to school for a year with his annual donation.

"And consider bright-colored hats sent to Afghanistan. No one can wear them. It makes a person a sniper target in a war zone to wear such a hat. I feel when we send aid to other countries, especially in the developing world, we must take the time to look at their greatest need and then try to fill it in ways that honor the culture. Financial aid is often the most pressing need."

In her shop, Bente takes knitting on consignment, and the profits go to charity. As these items sell, she can support different charities with a financial gift. Local soup kitchens, safe houses, and drug rehab centers as well as cancer patients and newborns are among the beneficiaries. Bente helps knitting find a home too. One knitter came in with a pile of scarves she wanted to place in the hands of the homeless. Bente helped by being the clearinghouse. She collected the lovely scarves and made sure they got to the local soup kitchen along with a check that month.

Bente's system creates many winners. Knitters make any knitted item they desire. Bente gets more traffic through her shop from knitters looking for supplies and shoppers looking for treasures. And local charities get a financial boost. There are many ways to knit for charity, and Bente reveals that sometimes the answers are unexpected.

Find out if your local yarn store has charity activities. Chances are they do, and you can get involved in your own community.

Going to the Dogs and Cats

Many humane shelters across the country have knitters working to keep the animals in their care warm and happy. Thousands of animals come through shelters each year. It is a big job to find homes for all of them. And keeping the critters comfortable while they wait is important too.

Cat and dog lovers alike will find a place for their knitting at humane societies. Shelters need knitted mats for these animals to rest on while in their cages. And then when they are adopted, riding to their new home on a mat knit with love eases the transition. Animal lovers find that this is a great way to use up their odds and ends of yarn and help out a favorite charity.

Check your local humane society and see what their needs are. They can give you the measurements for the size mats they require. If they don't have a program in place, maybe you can suggest this as a great way to comfort the homeless animals. This is also a particularly easy project for children to get involved in.

Local to international organizations offer many ways to knit for charity. But what other ways are there to enjoy this craft and share it with others? Many ideas spring from the inventive hearts of knitters. Read the next chapter and find out more ways to spread love with your needles.

7

Increase

Outreach

Increase: to create a new stitch in the middle of your knitting.

Knitters always have something on their needles. In fact, the queue of projects gets pretty long with all those tempting yarns. Organizations in need of knitting abound. Many were discussed in chapter 6. Family and friends get handcrafted gifts from knitters. And still there are more ways to share your knitting. The stories and ideas in this chapter focus on unique ways to think of sharing your craft, not necessarily through a national or local organization but through your own ingenuity. You rejoice in the gift of knitting in your life. Now let's increase ways to spread the joy in unexpected places. Don't miss the loving opportunities right under your needles.

Fifty Scarves

The outreach pastor of our church leads a group working in the local soup kitchen. Winter is a busy time for comforting outreach. Even in Northern California, winter is cold. Our pastor saw a need and asked the Stitches of Love knitting group at church to make him fifty scarves. He didn't put in a request to a national knitting charity because he knew there were knitters in his own congregation willing to help. He saw a need and went into action.

Scarves are so simple that anyone in our church group could make one. We got to work. We tried out new patterns and fresh yarn. We knit all spring and summer. Come fall we had passed our quota and were able to present the outreach group with seventy-six scarves. This may be a one-time effort, or we may continue to make scarves. Seeing a need and reaching out is simple enough. Take a chance. You don't have to clothe every homeless person you see, but how nice to offer a warm scarf rather than walk on by. Look in your community with fresh eyes and maybe you'll find a need your gift of knitting can fill. Many national knitting charities started as small grassroots efforts. Who knows where your needles will take you.

Crazy Garter Scarf Pattern

Here's one of the popular scarf patterns our Stitches of Love group used to meet our fifty-scarf quota. You may find it's a fun one to try. This crazy garter scarf is knit long-ways and works up so fast. You can change the cast-on number to adjust the length of the scarf. Casting on 150 is a good starting point, but it's fun to go as high as 200 or 300 for a longer creation.

Select a bulky yarn with a gauge of two or three stitches to the inch. Pick out five different colors. Cast on 150 stitches. This gives you about a fifty-inch scarf. Now knit every row until you run out of yarn. Attach the next color, even in the middle of a row, and keep knitting. Add each new color as the old one runs out. With the last color, be sure to save enough for the bind off, about four lengths of the total scarf. Bind off, weave in the ends, and share with a friend.

The Great Sock Lottery

When I knit my first sock, it was a revelation. It was not hard at all. I was stunned. I had avoided socks for years thinking they were beyond my level of expertise. However, when you break the pattern down into each section, just like a sweater, the sock comes together. Okay, so my first effort was not a pair as much as two socks made from the same yarn. One was noticeably smaller than the other. Still, I was hooked. I had conquered the impossible. Never mind that Red Cross volunteers had made millions. Never mind that the first unearthed knitted item was a sock. *I* had finally knit a sock. Now this was news.

In the first month of my newfound skill, I made four pairs, and yes, they started to match and look pretty good. I wanted to try out all kinds of yarn and rib patterns. The possibilities were endless. A silly idea popped into my head: I'll make socks for every family member and all my friends. Quickly a list formed in my head, and it grew pretty long. I could never make that many pairs of socks. And how would I choose who got the first pair? The next instant the Great Sock Lottery was born. My New Year's resolution: each month knit a pair of socks for a person selected at random.

I mailed off invitations and entry forms to forty-eight people. Not everyone entered, but I received twenty-three responses, plenty to keep me busy. Each month I drew a name. While knitting, I spent time thinking and praying for this dear person and then mailed them a surprise. It was great fun to mail a box with a return address from the Great Sock Lottery. I even started including a mesh laundry bag so these handmade beauties would last in the laundry. Don't put them in the dryer!

On the next page there is an invitation you can use to start your own Great Sock Lottery.

The Stash

Overheard at a recent yarn sale: "My stash is so important that I have placed it in my will. That should tell you how

You Are Invited

Enter the Great Sock Lottery

I am a crazy knitter who has learned to make socks.

If you would like a chance to win a pair of handmade socks, fill out the enclosed entry form and mail it back by January 5. Every month this year I will select a name and knit a custom pair of socks.

How to Measure Your Foot

First, use a tape measure to find the circumference of the ball of your foot (all the way around the fattest part down by your toes). Next, measure the length of your foot. Place the tape measure on the floor starting at the wall. Stand on the tape measure. Where does your big toe hit? That's how long your foot is.

Favorite Colors

When deciding on a color choice, be as specific as you can. Green is fine, but do you prefer forest green, lime green, or kelly green? Just blue? Or baby blue, turquoise blue, cobalt blue? See what I mean?

Name _____

Foot measurements

    Ball of foot _____ inches

    Length of foot _____ inches

Favorite color #1 _____

Favorite color #2 _____

big it is." Yikes! I don't wish the woman harm, but oh to be heir to angora.

As a novice I did not understand "the stash." Why on earth are these knitters buying more yarn when they have a perfectly good project at home? Silly newbie. Once you've "tasted" cashmere, it's hard to go back to a diet of acrylic. The scratch on your hands only reminds you there are softer fibers to enjoy. So the stash begins.

Knitters collect yarn for all sorts of reasons: waiting for the perfect pattern to arise or because this ultrasoft skein in this luscious color needs a good home. Your stash grows as you can afford space and dollars. Ah, the joys of a yarn sale! The first thing you do is touch. Before you know it, you've done it again—purchased yarn to start another brand-new project. The queue of works in progress gets longer and longer.

Managing the stash is something most knitters eventually must consider. Sometimes it gets overwhelming. In the beginning, you just add a few extra balls here and there. But soon your stash has grown to proportions you never thought possible. Gale has an epic stash. She buys carefully but in quantity so she will not run out midproject. And she always has several projects going. The Ravelry website calculates yardage. Gale recently discovered she has 126 *miles* of yarn! For me, just filling two packing boxes was enough for me to take stock. Some knitters may wait until an entire room is full.

Rethinking your purchases, you discover you cannot knit all you have collected. Once must-have yarns lose their appeal. Colors you thought you'd never tire of look dull. Or you've waited so long to make a garment that it's gone out of style or the child has grown to adulthood. What to do? You have great yarn you want to hold on to forever, yet there isn't room for more. Consider letting go.

One way to manage the yarn overflow is to have a stash bash. If you belong to a knitting circle, you already have a willing group. If you don't have a regular knitting group, think of the people you know who knit or whom you've met at your local yarn shop. It's time for a party. Invite knitters for a yarn swap. You can use yarn as currency. Whatever you put in you get to take out. Though this doesn't exactly decrease your stash, it does change the colors and fiber content.

Another way to run the bash is to sell yarn. Pile the yarn by price or fiber content. Since the purpose is to get rid of the balls you're willing to part with, keep the prices low. You can even have a free bin to tempt other knitters into taking your yarn. Of course you'll probably rummage for goodies too.

A stash bash may appear to be just moving yarn from one stash to another. To really get rid of yarn, consider other methods of finding new homes for your treasures. Every so often I mail yarn to a knitting friend. I routinely discover that my stash of sock yarn is enough to outfit an army. If I want new colors, I have to make room. So off it goes. What a surprise to get a ball or two in the mail.

Other outlets for your bulging stash are schools and organizations needing yarn. Waldorf schools teach each student to knit and always need yarn. Girl Scout troops are often looking for craft supplies. Schoolteachers need yarn too. Is there a community center searching for supplies? Think about new homes for your stash. Of course, this means there will be more room for you to buy new treasures. It's a win-win situation.

A Servant Heart

I am hooked on socks. I love all the steps. It's magic every time I turn a heel. I'm stunned every time the kitchener stitch works when I graft the toe together. I love it all. I keep finding more people who need socks.

Remember the story of Jesus washing the feet of his disciples? He is the servant caring for their basic needs. And as always, Jesus gives a greater meaning to a simple task. There are no small deeds in this world. Fill the world with little acts of loving-kindness. This is my mission. I have taken this story as my own when thinking of making socks. I love to wrap my friends and family in hand-knits, and I knit for various charities, but what about other people? Those I have a nodding acquaintance with, people who serve me and I'd like to thank in a concrete way. Whose feet could I "wash"?

I got to thinking about this and started making a list of people who need a surprise gift of socks. First, my hairdresser. He's on his feet all day long. I made a thick pair of slipper socks for him to wear when he gets home. Next came a favorite waitress. I see her once a month when I take myself out to lunch. She's on her feet all day too. I made a pair of anklets with a lacy cuff. They were her tip one day. Who else is standing all day? The checker at the grocery store. My mailman. The list started to grow. I would be busy. I want these people to know someone sees their work, someone knows they have tired feet. I feel God's pleasure when I am his hands. He smiles when I get one of his lessons right. I have a whole lot of learning to do, but I understand small acts of loving-kindness.

Whom can you surprise with a knitted gift? Scarves knit up so quickly. Make a few comfy scarves you can hand out when the spirit strikes you. Once you get started you may find there are many people you'd like to cover in warm, fuzzy thoughts. Give it a go; you'll be surprised by the results.

A hiker you pass on your daily walk.

A tired mom you see often in the park.

A repairman who services your home.

The list will grow.

Slip-Stitch Scarf Pattern

If you are trying to find an easy yet interesting gift to make for an unexpected person, try this elegant slip-stitch pattern. And it's reversible! Cast on any multiple of four plus three. Try twenty-three stitches. Row 1: knit three, then with yarn in front slip next stitch purl wise return yarn to back. Repeat to last three stitches and knit those three. Row 2: knit one, then with yarn in front slip next stitch purl wise return yarn to back, knit three. Repeat to last stitch and knit that one. Repeat rows one and two until scarf is the desired length and bind off.

Yarnbombing

It's dark, but I can see thanks to the streetlight shining down on me. My hands are shaking. Quickly I wrap the knitted strip around the tree trunk and start to stitch it closed, locking it in place. It takes two minutes tops. I turn and rush back up the driveway into the safety of my own house. I wasn't doing anything more destructive than posting a sign for an upcoming garage sale, but putting a cozy on the tree in the corner of my yard felt sneaky. The next day I felt silly when no one noticed, not even my son on the way to school. So in broad daylight I wrapped the tree with a second bigger piece of knitting. Now I had visions of wrapping trees up and down my street and going by my friends' houses and wrapping some of their trees.

Why this strange knitting urge? I read about yarnbombing and decided to give it a try. My attempt was tiny compared to the big things being bombed across the globe. Knitta, a group in Texas, started this phenomenon. One day a bored shop owner knit a little cozy for the door handle of her shop. She got a fun response and decided to wrap the tree outside her shop as well. A new kind of urban tagging was born. Now everything from trees and buses to an entire abandoned gas station has been wrapped in knitting and crochet. Why? Well, it's fun for one thing. And it certainly softens the world. Weaving hearts of yarn into a fence around a vacant lot brings a smile to those passing by. For some yarnbombers, there is more to it, a bigger statement perhaps. For me, it was for the smile alone. I tagged three trees on my street this summer. It made me giggle to see them as I motored by.

Yarnbombing is not a permanent thing, however. The rains came. My knitting grew soggy and ended up around the bottom of the trees. It was a silly experiment and fun while it lasted. Yarnbombing is a unique way to get rid of odd balls of yarn clutter, and it brightens your neighborhood for a season. You might want to start under cover of darkness like I did or be brave and step out in broad daylight. Either way, have a giggle and see what happens.

———

The stories and projects in this chapter hopefully nudged you to take a fresh look at what you can do with your knitting. In the next chapter, we'll see what others have been up to already. We'll see the ways knitters are both building and serving their communities.

8

Work in the Round

Community

Work in the round: a technique used for sleeves, socks, and neckbands that uses circular or double pointed needles so the ends of your knitting are joined and create a tube.

Quietly throughout the world, knitters are going about their craft with love and care. They sit in circles and stitch together. They knit alone and behind the scenes. One of my greatest pleasures is to hear what others are up to in the fiber world. It's encouraging and inspiring to find stories in the knitting circle, whether it's an individual with a new venture or an established group with years of service. Taking note of these acts of loving-kindness renews our faith and helps us continue our own acts of gentle service.

In this chapter, you will find what other knitters have done to use their craft to share their faith, build community, and make a difference. Maybe one of these stories will spark an idea in you to try something new with your knitting for others.

Knitwits

I wondered just how many knitting groups call themselves Knitwits. I found 51,700 hits when I typed it into Google. Yikes! We love the name. Makes us smile with silliness. One Knitwit group meets at Hillsboro High School in Nashville, Tennessee.

Sally Swor, a guidance counselor at Hillsboro, wanted to think of new ways to engage students. As a knitter, she decided to start a knitting club during the lunch break. Knitwits was born. Soon Sally had girls and guys, jocks and academics all sitting around clicking sticks together. Any given week, fifteen to twenty-five students knit during their lunch hour. Sometimes a few would show up, learn, and then take the skill out to their circle of friends. Knitting was not an activity confined to a single lunch hour. In fact, it became so popular that some teachers put up signs in their classrooms: No Food, No Drink, No Knitting. This may have stopped students from knitting in class, but it didn't dampen their spirit. The sticks kept flying.

In Knitwits, students can let down their guard a little and relax. High school is a stressful place, and knitting offers a release. There is no homework, just needlework.

In a campus culture where knitting is cool, it's hard not to join the fun. Becky Peterson, French teacher and lapsed knitter, credits Sally with getting her going again. She joined the group on occasion. When Sally retired, Becky inherited the Knitwits and became their faculty advisor. "It's just so dear to see these kids knitting. It's a real stress release for everyone."

As any teacher will tell you, keeping students engaged can be a tough job and not just in the classroom. Having fun is a worthy pursuit, but having a goal and purpose will keep kids coming back for more. Hillsboro High meets the needs of its community in many ways. During the holiday season, they run the successful Edgehill Angel Tree Project. For over twenty years, this project has offered students a way to serve. Each homeroom class is encouraged to adopt a child in the community. They collect money and donations during the fall semester and at Christmastime are able to provide food and gifts for the family of the child they've adopted. The Knitwits saw a chance to add a personal touch. They make hats and scarves to add to the gifts sent to each family.

Then one summer Dave Young, Hillsboro history teacher and track coach, spent some time in Vietnam, and he saw another opportunity for his students. Teachers, especially the good ones, always seem to have their students in mind. *How can I reach them and give them more?* Dave saw a need in Vietnam and knew his students could organize to help in a big way. He came home with the seeds of an idea.

Hillsboro High and Saigon Children Charity began their partnership in the 2003–4 school year. By the next school year, Hillsboro had raised $11,875, tripling their contribution from the year before. Initially, the school sponsored forty-one Vietnamese students. Now well over one hundred receive assistance each year. It takes $75 a year to sponsor a child. That money covers the cost of a school uniform and school supplies. Each family also gets twenty-two pounds of rice a month. In addition to sponsoring students, Hillsboro has raised enough money to construct two schools in southern Vietnam: Hillsboro High East and West.

Obviously, this charity work involves a school-wide effort with many ways of raising money. The Knitwits started contributing by selling their wares at a local yarn shop. They wanted to do more. Now each year they sponsor a live auction. The group selects a local venue, usually a restaurant, and stages a fashion show. While patrons (lots of parents, of course) dine, the kids model their creations, from hats and scarves to flower pins and mittens. The Knitwits literally sell the wares off their backs.

A knitting group at lunchtime. Children in need half a world away. A couple simple ideas from a few creative teachers offered up to a willing student body. Imagine if all the Knitwit groups I googled were as productive as the Knitwits at Hillsboro High School. Now that would be a force of great power.

Maximum Security Knitting

Judy Ditmore never thought she'd end up in prison one day. She went in with yarn and came out with beautiful hand-knit sweaters. Judy, upstanding citizen and fiber artist, tells how she started a prison knitting program.

"This just fell in my lap. In 1998, some people at Colorado Correctional Industries (CCI) had a good idea: start a knitting program for the women's prison in Canyon City, Colorado. The idea: provide offenders with an activity to build self-esteem and create jobs. The prison was interested but couldn't offer any money for the program. So CCI approached local yarn stores to see if they'd be interested in getting involved. Unfortunately, none of the shop owners had the time. Like any small business, running a yarn shop leaves little time for extras. Eventually, my name came up. I had recently sold my shop to become a wholesaler.

"The project was not going to be a charity operation; it would be a business proposition. I needed samples of my yarns knit to showcase at trade shows. The plan developed for the offenders to knit with my yarns. I then took the samples on the road. It's quite a leap to go from no knitting experience to creating high-quality samples. There were many steps in between to give the women the required skills.

"CCI and I did a lot of research to get things going. First, we developed a business plan. We outlined the program in detail, from the work the women would do to the pay scales. For example, we had to research knitting needles to find some suitable for prison use. We discovered Boye Baleen needles. Baleen is a kind of plastic that can't be melted. You can't put a needle in a light socket and melt it into a weapon. And they are *not* hollow. This was an important feature. The prison officials needed to be sure we were not smuggling cocaine into the prison through the knitting needles.

"Before we worked in the prison, we took a class about procedures and expectations. We learned all kinds of things. Instructors told us, 'Bring nothing in and take nothing out, and you'll do fine.' Of course, I brought in knitting supplies and took out finished products. But I couldn't, for example, bring in a gift card or take out a letter to mail. This safeguarded us from getting caught up in inmate dramas.

"We also learned a lot about sexual harassment. Just leaning over an inmate's shoulder—say, to demonstrate a knitting stitch—was considered sexual harassment. Knitting is a hands-on skill, so it was really hard for me to not take the knitting needles from someone's hands to demonstrate. At first it was very awkward. I am a touchy-feely kind of person, and now I had to be very conscious of my interactions with these women.

"To get the program going, I went to the prison three times a week for eighteen months. I held classes from nine to three. Every hour a new group of eight to ten women came in. I taught over sixty-five women to knit. Eventually, about ten women had the skill to work for me full-time. Of course, they had the time to work twenty-four hours a day, but usually they worked eight to ten hours on their knitting. The prison even upgraded the recreation room for them, putting in special lighting and comfortable chairs. Some of the women took knitting to their rooms, but they could have only one or two pieces of a garment at a time. If they could put an entire garment together, they could wear it and walk out. You see, I was there three days a week wearing hand-knits. Others were in and out with me. The guards didn't want an inmate to blend in and escape.

"I paid the women $1.50 an hour or by the piece, and I paid $12.00 for a completed shawl or sweater. That sounds like slave labor; however, other prison jobs paid only 38 cents an hour. At correctional facilities in Colorado, the women have to pay for many of their own needs: shampoo, hygiene supplies, phone calls, and the like. The women who worked for me were the elite of the prison, high wage earners.

"Since I could not pay more or bring any gifts for individuals, I purchased knitting books for the prison library. Those who wanted to expand their expertise learned more from the books. Three of the women turned into tremendous knitters. They kept learning and did a lot of work for me.

"The knit program meant extra work for the guards. The women could have only one ball of yarn in their room at a time. If they needed more, they had to go to the guard and ask for the next ball. It was difficult for the guards to keep track of everything—who was working on which project and so forth. And the guards delivered the finished projects to me. On more than one occasion I paid for a garment only to find it incomplete. The knitter worked just three-quarters of the sleeves and folded and bagged the garment, presenting it as finished. The guard accepted it and passed it on to me. Sometimes a month went by before I needed to open the package, and I'd find the mistake. Because of these kinds of problems, the program lasted only two years at the maximum-security facility. We switched to a minimum-security facility and continued the program. However, the Canyon City Women's Prison still has about sixty knitters. The group switched to knitting for free. They work on items for Project Linus and

Warm Up America! I'm happy to know they are still knitting. As you know, once you learn, it's hard *not* to knit.

"The program proved to be very good at its goal: to raise an offender's self-esteem and create jobs. The thing I am most proud of, though, is that the women found a new community of friends. I've kept in touch with some of the knitters who've gotten out. Some have joined local knitting guilds. There they meet women from all walks of life. They become friends with women they never would have come in contact with otherwise. Knitting opens up a whole new way to communicate. They build healthy friendships and enrich their lives."

Hundreds of Hats

As a young bride expecting her first baby, Marge Pangborn decided to put her dormant knitting skills to use. Marge's grandma had taught her to knit when she was five. Marge knit again in high school during the argyle sock craze. But now it was time to knit for her firstborn. Living in the Philippines, where her husband was stationed with the Air Force, Marge wrote home to her mom and aunt asking for knitting supplies. "I made a blanket for my son and then even attempted a sweater for my husband. I found I really enjoyed knitting, and I had plenty of time on my hands where I was."

After they returned to the States, her knitting passion grew. Marge discovered Mary Maxim patterns and embarked on knitting a sweater for everyone in her extended family. Mary Maxim patterns feature intarsia color work. Marge knit sweaters covered with bears, lambs, planes, pheasants, all kinds of things. "I even remember doing one for a nurse in the hospital when I gave birth to our only daughter. I sold it to the nurse for five dollars. Can you imagine? I still have the original list of sweaters I knit for family and friends back in the 1950s—157 sweaters! Truly my passion."

During the years of raising her family and working full-time, Marge still relaxed in the evenings with her knitting. These days she and her husband live in Georgia. "We attend a very missions-minded church where a variety of opportunities opened up for my knitting. I want to pay tribute to my grandma who taught me to knit. So I take pictures of my work and record it all in an album." Marge has quite an extensive list of where her work goes. Slippers to Asia and Russia. Sweaters and socks to the Czech Republic. Blankets to Hurricane Katrina victims. And hats. Hundreds of hats. Hats to Uruguay, Appalachia, Phoenix, Lawrenceville, Ukraine, and Belarus.

"When I complete a hat, I hold it open and pray that the future owner of the hat will come to know Jesus as their Savior. I pray they will ask forgiveness for their sins and invite Jesus into their heart and life. I also pray I'll see the future owner of the hat in heaven someday. I knit helmets of salvation. The Lord definitely showed me he wanted me to do this. What a privilege."

Word of Mouth

Ann Ellington Wagner is an enthusiastic knitter. A holiday trip to the Pink Palace Museum in Memphis got her started on a whole new knitting adventure.

The Pink Palace Museum is a place where visitors explore a large collection of permanent exhibits about the natural and cultural history of Memphis. The palace is quite a sight, a mansion built of pink Georgian marble in the early 1920s. The home was designed for Clarence Saunders, founder of the Piggly Wiggly grocery chain. Before completion, however, Saunders went bankrupt. In the late 1920s, the home was given to the city of Memphis to be used as a museum.

The Pink Palace has a Christmas tradition. For over fifty years, it has held an annual holiday fund-raiser called the Enchanted Forest. This festival of trees started in the basement of a local department store and has grown to include automated teddy bears and elves, a gingerbread village, holidays around the world, and a penguin pond. The dozens of evergreens are the big draw. Trees are sponsored and decorated by local businesses, churches, and volunteers to transform the Pink Palace into an Enchanted Forest. Many of the sponsored trees raise money for charity, and the decorations are given away after the event. In 2008, Ann Ellington Wagner and her youngest daughter went for a visit.

Ann tells the story.

"The festival of trees was quite a sight. We came up the escalator and saw the most beautiful tree. It was decorated with tiny caps, little booties and mittens, and equally small blankets. It just brought me to tears. And it gave me an idea.

"I am the special projects chairman at the Ellington Agriculture Center in Nashville. The center was named for my father, a two-term governor of Tennessee. I called our commissioner of agriculture and asked him if we could bring the festival of trees idea to our museum. We'd start small of course: one tree. I wanted to sponsor a tree at the annual Christmas open house we hold at the museum. He gave me a green light, and so I had to find knitters.

"I put an article in my church's bulletin and got three knitters. I found another knitter in a doctor's waiting room. When she asked what I was working on, it led me right into my speech. My oldest daughter crochets, and she began working on blankets. While crocheting on her lunch break, she got two more women to join the project. Then a knitting group some fifty miles from Nashville heard about our project and asked if they could help. Sure! Next a spinner who demonstrates at the agriculture museum gave me twenty-one cap and bootie sets. Word of mouth decorated our beautiful tree with little works of love. I even decorated wooden clothespins for attaching the garments to the branches of the tree. It was beautiful.

"We invited all the knitters and crocheters to gather at our December open house and acknowledged their work. The tree even got coverage in the local paper. I am praying this first tree will lead to having a tree each year. We donated the items to a hospital with a neonatal wing. It is my dream that one day we may rival the Pink Palace with trees of every sort. This word-of-mouth knitting project already has done a lot of good."

You Add a Row

In May of 2000, Susan Mock opened the Stitchin' Den in Estes Park, Colorado. Estes Park is a lovely mountain town north of Denver. This small community with lots of heart welcomes nearly five million visitors every year, as it is a gateway to Rocky Mountain National Park. Tourists fill the town all summer. There is a national rodeo in August, and the Fourth of July is a bit of Americana not to be missed. In the fall there's great hiking, and in the winter there is skiing and snowshoeing. And all year long there are spectacular views. It's a great place to sit and knit.

Susan Mock reached out to the community from the beginning. She wanted to include not just the fiber friends she was supplying with knitting, needlepoint, and cross-stitch yarns but the community at large. Susan started a program called Happy Stitches. She'd seen this done in other knit shops and was eager to try it. If you visit Estes Park, you may discover a basket with an intriguing note attached:

Happy Stitches

This program puts knitting baskets in popular resting spots around Estes Park. We invite you to sit and knit for a bit and leave the project for the next person to add their touch. When all is said and done (or when the scarf is long enough), these projects will be collected and donated around Estes Park. We want to thank you for helping us make someone happy!

What a delight. I found one of Susan's baskets when I was on vacation in Estes Park. Knitting is the perfect activity for a lazy summer afternoon while sipping coffee and looking out at the Rockies. Susan says it's difficult to keep the baskets full in the summer. So many people find joy in adding a row. The scarves pile up. I contacted Susan to ask her more about her Happy Stitches baskets, and I learned that the baskets are just part of a busy charity knitting enterprise. Susan told me about many other things she does through the Stitchin' Den.

"We have many local customers, but we also get lots of travelers. We help them all. Sometimes a knitter on the road has run out of supplies or wants to start a new project. Or someone wanders in not having knit in years, but vacation opens up time and they want to start again. We have so many different people coming through the shop, and they bring all kinds of ideas from across the country. We support all kinds of charities, whatever our customers are into. Sometimes it feels a little schizophrenic, but we get involved in lots of endeavors. We've done pink knitting for Susan G. Komen for the Cure. There's *Guideposts* Knit for Kids and Warm Up America! as well as Warm the World. Right now with the gulf oil spill in the news, we've got customers wanting to help through knitting. We are putting together washcloths to help with the cleanup of critters. The cloths can be used only once, so they'll need thousands. I love it that our community finds knitted ways to answer needs. It's wonderful to be a part of such creative solutions.

"There is such solidarity in the knitting community. So many lovely people all doing a wide variety of things to make the world a better place. I love it that our shop can help them. Fiber arts bring people together. I've pulled out my knitting on a bus in a foreign country and had 'conversations' with people, though we don't speak the same language.

"Knitting creates community as well as being a way to give back. We donate a lot of yarn. We give to senior centers and Girl Scout troops, even individuals if they come in with a charity project they want to pursue. We also donate our time teaching people to knit. When a school needs yarn for projects, they often also need someone to help teach the kids to knit. From our little shop all the way up through vendors and the National Needlearts Association (TNNA), the fiber community is willing to donate yarn to help make these projects happen. I think if politicians picked up knitting, a lot of problems could get solved faster."

Susan and the knitters in her shop are certainly doing their part to answer life's tangled needs with knitting.

Knit a River

The mission of WaterAid, a global charity, is to overcome poverty by enabling the world's poorest people to gain access to safe water, sanitation, and hygiene education. In 2006, the I Knit shop in London teamed up with WaterAid to create a dramatic petition. Thousands of knitters from London and the United States to Japan and Australia began producing blue knitted patches. Squares poured into WaterAid headquarters.

In possibly the largest knitted project ever undertaken, an estimated one hundred thousand pieces were sewn together to create a dramatic display and an impassioned plea. The knitted river's sole purpose: to travel to WaterAid events and attract attention to their cause. On July 14, 2007, the river was draped from the rooftop of the National Theatre on London's South Bank as part of the theatre's annual Watch This Space festival. It was quite the conversation starter. WaterAid volunteers engaged passersby and handed out information about the End Water Poverty campaign.

The river has traveled to many events throughout Europe. One of its most spectacular displays came in May of 2007 just before the G8 summit in Germany. Two hundred knitters and WaterAid supporters carried a portion of the knitted river through London into Parliament Square and Whitehall, the home of the British government, where the meeting was taking place. A small section was handed over to the prime minister at 10 Downing Street, calling for pressure on the G8 to end water poverty. This dramatic project helps WaterAid spread its message.

While the knitting project is not accepting more squares, you can find out more about WaterAid at wateraid.org. There you will find ways to be involved from the local to the global level.

Childbirth Instruction

Charleen McWilliam had a unique request. "I need someone to knit me a uterus." Knit a uterus. Really? "I've got the pattern but not the knitting skills." Why exactly did she need a knitted uterus? Good question. Here's what happened.

"I work with LifeWind International coordinating the Women's Health Program. LifeWind is a holistic ministry meeting physical and spiritual needs. We work to bring lasting change, not temporary relief. LifeWind is in ninety countries throughout the world. I work in Latin America, Ethiopia, Africa, Southeast Asia, Haiti, and most recently Delhi, India.

"I train national women leaders; I call them champions. These women then train other women in communities within their country, who then go neighbor to neighbor, visiting and teaching individual women how to care for themselves and their families. We teach many subjects, such as nutrition, sanitation, hygiene, how to care for themselves during pregnancy, how to recognize complications, and what to do and where to go.

"My ministry with LifeWind is supported by Valley Church in Cupertino, California. One of the ways Valley Church supports its missionaries is by making sure each one has a representative in the congregation. These people serve as our connection. So when I needed a knitter, I asked my representative if anyone at Valley could make a uterus. An odd request, I know. But the medical models I'd found on the market each cost thirty-five dollars, too much for my limited budget. I'd been searching for alternatives and found a pattern for a knitted uterus. What a great solution. It's lightweight and would travel well, smashed in a suitcase. Now I needed someone to make them.

"Erika Luginbuhl was willing to give the unusual project a try. It was such a strange pattern, and Erika wasn't quite sure she got it right. So she tried a second time, modifying it a little. The second one she made was a C-section model. Erika knew what she was looking for because she had been a midwife. Erika sent me both knitted models. They were great, just what I needed. I put in an order for more. In two weeks, Erika produced a dozen uteri. Our partnership blossomed.

"It's difficult, coming from our culture, to understand how informative this visual aid is to these women. They have no idea how their bodies are made or what really happens in childbirth. The biggest problem of all is they do not understand the complications of childbirth and how serious some of them are. One of the major killers of women in the developing world is hemorrhage during childbirth. The model shows them that the uterus is a large muscle composed of many blood vessels. If it tears or doesn't get hard (contract), they will lose too much blood and bleed to death. It dynamically teaches them and makes a big difference in their lives. Such a small thing, but what a difference it means to a family of poverty. Families suffer so much from the loss of the mother of the family.

"This is a grassroots ministry filtering down to small communities. The uterus model is used in a home visit to explain to a pregnant woman the childbirth process and possible complications. Sometimes it is used in a class in the village. The models come complete with a baby doll from their country. We leave the uterus for future education. We even include a pattern so that with Erika's sample they are able to make more. Erika's ministry of knitting a uterus—and there are so many of them now—has literally reached the world."

I contacted Erika to hear about her side of this partnership with Charleen.

Erika has been knitting uteri for several years. Anytime Charleen runs out, she puts in an order for a few more. It makes for some interesting conversations when Erika pulls out this knitting project. Someone will ask what she's making. "No, it's not a sock. It's a uterus. See, this is the cervix that opens up in childbirth." Oh my. Erika is a proper lady, and it gives her a giggle to say this. She also says it's funny to see the wild colors of her donated yarn. Striped or bright orange—it doesn't matter. It all gets knit up. Erika has many outlets for her charity knitting, but these knitted uteri are the most unique by far. "My mother taught me to knit when I was three or four years old. Now I'm an old woman, and God is using this talent for ministry. Who would have thought my knitting would provide such a much-needed service?" Or have such far-reaching effects!

Knitting Olympics

Knitters belong to a worldwide community. Whenever I knit in public, someone will make a comment. Often a person will tell me about how a grandma or an aunt knit all the time. Other times a fellow knitter will ask what I'm working on and even pull out her own project of the moment. Knitters speak the same language: love of craft. Knitting promotes community in many ways. Knitters rally for causes like wartime efforts. We gather for celebrations like baby showers. We meet for comfort in weekly knit sessions. And we get together for fun and even silliness. We are a community.

In 2006, the Winter Olympics were in Torino, Italy. No one I knew got to go to the games. But there was a knitter with a crazy idea that caught on: the Knitting Olympics. Stephanie Pearl-McPhee, aka the Yarn Harlot, issued a challenge from her blog: cast on a project during the opening ceremonies and finish by the time the Olympic flame goes out sixteen days later. The idea was to stretch yourself as a knitter using an Olympic effort to work through the challenge. Knitters emailed their plans. Everyone who finished their project would get a chance to win a prize in a drawing from Stephanie. But the real joy, of course, was knowing that you completed the challenge.

The community got into gear, and 4,071 knitters entered and warmed up their needles. Silly? Maybe. Community building? You bet. Knitting for sixteen days to complete a challenging project certainly generated comments from those watching the knitters work. What's the point? Well, fun and games to be sure. But the Olympics capture our attention for sixteen days each time they roll around, and we are all one community. I think the Knitting Olympics reminded knitters they are a worldwide community, a crazy group maybe but one that tackles big tasks with humor.

Needles heated up again for the 2010 Olympics in Vancouver, Canada. This time even more knitters signed up. International teams formed. The excitement required the work of many people to help Stephanie pull it off. Looks like the Knitting Olympics is here to stay. Start training for 2014!

Electives

Elizabeth Claverie is a seventh-grade English teacher at a Catholic middle school. Several years ago the staff started offering electives to their students. They knew education goes beyond just reading, writing, and arithmetic. The kids needed more. Of course, there was no budget, so the staff came up with a variety of classes they could teach themselves. The rotating selection over the years has included gardening, cooking, ballroom dancing, a virtual trip to Spain, and more. Elizabeth taught all kinds of things. She has settled on ballroom dancing and knitting. (No, not at the same time, but who knows. Elizabeth encourages all kinds of creative expressions.) Elizabeth talks about the knitting elective.

"I learned to knit about four years ago. My roommate knit, and so I asked her to show me how. She knit in the continental style. I could not grasp it. I tried and tried. I eventually gave up and found the American style. That I could figure out. Then I was off. I knit scarves, all kinds of scarves. Once I got the hang of knitting, I enjoyed stretching the creative possibilities. I got bored with the same old thing, so I'd weave in unusual yarns. I'd make really long fringe. Or I'd make the whole scarf really long. It was fun. I don't have a desire to make sweaters. I am good and fast at scarves.

"When the school decided to offer electives, I'd been knitting for about a year. I thought I could probably teach the kids to knit. Thirty-six students signed up the first time! Happily, several moms offered to help. Teaching knitting is a very one-on-one activity. Some kids picked it up quickly and began teaching the others. That is just the kind of thing I love to see.

"I was surprised by the enthusiastic response. The kids loved it. Wednesday electives got to be almost a therapy time. The kids chatted and knitted. There was no agenda. It was a free time just to relax. I didn't force anyone to knit. I didn't want to do anything that would make them hate it. Some kids just needed the space to sit quietly for a while. Eventually, though, they were intrigued enough to learn how to knit. In the end, everyone in the class was knitting. In fact, it got to the point where kids would ask if they could knit in their regular classes. I always let them as long as they finished their schoolwork. I know many kids listened more attentively while they knit.

"The project of choice in the elective was a scarf. Some of the kids got so good they knit hats as well. No one had to finish a project to pass the class. This was a time for them to learn a new skill, not be graded on the outcome. I called Catholic Charities CYO and asked if they could use our scarves. Patty said, 'Of course.' And at the end of the year, she came to collect the scarves the kids had made and took them to the homeless. We have a great picture of her sitting in the courtyard with her arms stretched out and draped with scarves. She was covered with scarves on her arms, neck, head, and lap. The kids were excited about their accomplishments.

"I had one kid, Giovanni, who took up knitting and would not let go. He started making a piece, and he loved it. But for reasons we could not figure out, he kept decreasing. He ended up with a strangely shaped piece. It started out as a rectangle, but one side kept decreasing into a triangle. He really wanted to donate his work and asked me what it could be. I figured out I could fold the rectangle sides together and sew them down and the triangle piece could flop over as a flap. It made an adorable little orange clutch purse. Giovanni was so proud of it. Patty took it when she came to collect the kids' knitting.

"Patty wrote back to the kids, letting them know how well received their knitted scarves were; she specifically mentioned Giovanni's purse. Apparently, Melissa, a mentally handicapped girl, loved the purse and carried it with her wherever she went—just the kind of thing you want to see come from this project. Good for both kids.

"The other part about the knitting class I loved was the opportunity it gave me to make references to God. I do this often in my English classes. I mentioned how they were knit together in their mother's womb. I see metaphor in so many things. Knitting is no different. It gave me a chance to give the kids little life lessons without banging them over the head with examples. So if someone was frustrated with learning to knit, I would point out that knitting is a step-by-step process that takes lots of time. I could reinforce how there are many worthwhile things that take lots of time. Knitting doesn't get done overnight. Or when they'd make a mistake in their knitting, I'd assure them it was no big deal. They could undo it and try again. It's a very gentle way to teach. It sinks in, and they remember it. The knitting elective is so much more than just learning to knit. I'm glad I am able to offer it to our kids."

It's fun to read about what knitters are doing and the many creative ways of making an impact. The more you knit, the more ways you find to make an impression on your world. And the more you knit, the more tips and tricks you pick up. In the next chapter, I'll share some of the knitting knowledge I've found helpful along the way.

9

Accessories

Tips, Books, and Websites

Accessories: knitting notions you need, such as scissors, tape measure, tapestry needles, stitch markers, point protectors, gauge guide, etc.

Knitting wisdom is acquired over time. As with any pursuit, work at it long enough and you will learn lots of secrets. Many knit tricks, good websites, and great books are passed along from one knitter to another. I've collected some here that are easy to share and nice to know about. Some of these things are time-honored ideas that have been floating around for a while; other bits may be new to you.

Joining a regular group can be one of the best ways to acquire knitting wisdom. But where are these groups? Maybe you'd like to start a knitting circle of your own. I've included how-tos to help you start your own knitting group. I hope you find some accessories here to make your knitting experience more enjoyable.

Tips and Tricks

• Start your next sweater with the sleeves. They are usually the quickest pieces to complete. You will know if you like the pattern and yarn much sooner. Some sweaters have design or construction reasons for working the pieces in a particular order, but usually you can start with any piece you like. Start small, smile sooner.

• For sleeves, the pattern reads, "Make two alike." It was a revelation to me to also make them *at the same time*. It takes a little planning, but it means there will be no second-guessing as to whether you have the right length for the second sleeve. Use two balls of yarn, one for each sleeve. Tie a different color bow of scrap yarn to each sleeve to keep track of which sleeve is which. When you are making a cardigan, you can also work the two front pieces at the same time.

• It happens. You have to unravel your knitting to fix a mistake and then put your work back on the needles. But taking stitches off the needles and putting them back on again can be nerve-racking. You don't want the entire thing to unravel.

Make it easier on yourself. Pick up the stitches on a needle one or two sizes smaller than your original work. The stitches will glide on, and then you can transfer them back to the size you need. Circulars work best for this, since you don't have to worry about which end to load and unload.

• Be brave and modify. Add button bands to a zipper design. Take button bands out and make it an open cardigan. Change colors, add accents, switch yarn combinations, alter the length. These are often simple changes that require a little preplanning to make them happen. If you want a second opinion on how to modify a pattern, ask your knitting group or someone at a local shop. Just remember, the project is yours, so change and create.

• Yarn sold in hanks needs to be wound into balls before you can knit with it, or it will become a tangled mess. The shop where you make your purchase will usually offer to wind the yarn for you. Or you can invest in a swift and ball winder. Of course, there is the old standby: ask a loved one to hold out their hands while you wind. Do this often enough, and they'll invest in the swift and ball winder for the next gift-giving occasion. (It worked at my house.)

• Copy your pattern and put the original aside to use again. This keeps your original legible. Now you can mark the pattern as you knit. Even if you are not one to write on patterns, having a copy means you can continue your work even if you misplace the working copy. Also, you will have a clean copy to make the project a second or third time if it's a favorite.

Finally, you can make note of any design changes you incorporated into your work.

• There's a lot of math involved in knitting: pattern repeats, yardage estimates, and needle sizes. But here's some knitting math you may not have heard about: pleasure per dollar. When you finally decide to go for it and buy the good stuff for your next project, you may be startled to discover that your new sweater costs $80 to $200, and at the moment it's just a pile of yarn. Okay, time for a pleasure per dollar analysis. Let's say you go to a movie and pay $10 for the ticket. Of course, you'll need munchies during the film, so add another $20. Now figure in a baby sitter: $30. So your movie night cost you $60 for three hours, or $20 per hour. (I didn't even add in parking or a husband or a friend coming along.) The average knitter takes sixty hours to make a sweater. Even with $180 worth of yarn, that's only $3 an hour. That's a good entertainment value. And extrasoft merino wool feels so good slipping over your fingers as you work.

• The tags from bread bags make great temporary bobbins. Wind up the tail you are saving to sew up the seam on a sleeve or side seam. This keeps it out of your way.

• Variegated yarn offers all kinds of design possibilities. But it can be hard to work with and very unpredictable. That's both the fun and the frustration of it. Take a look at your yarn. How often does the color change? Sometimes colors come in quick succession; other times there are long gradual changes. Each will give your piece a different look. The length of your rows also has an effect on how the colors knit up. Short rows take longer for the colors to change, and long rows appear to change often. Sometimes the colors pool; that is, they collect in blotches rather than blending in stripe or random patterns. One way to tame variegated yarn and prevent pooling is to use two skeins of yarn at the same time. Knit back and forth with one ball and then the other, carefully twisting the yarn when you switch. This will even out the effect of the yarn.

• When you are knitting for a charity, it is wise to check out where the work goes and who benefits from it. A friend of mine knit hats for babies at a local hospital. To her dismay she discovered the hospital was charging for the hats. The hospital was using the hats as a fund-raiser for their own projects. It's not a bad thing to raise money for much-needed projects, but it was not my friend's intention. She wanted to give those hats as a free gift to new parents.

• Circular needles make good stitch holders, especially for large groups of stitches. Use point protectors if you are worried the stitches will fall off as you work other sections. Another way to hold live stitches is to thread a piece of scrap yarn through, using a tapestry needle. Loop the yarn closed and tie a knot to keep your stitches from escaping.

• Never knit after 10:00 p.m. Let me clarify: never knit anything complex late at night. At my house, I am free to knit patterns until 10:00, but after that I have to switch to a mindless garter stitch or stockinette. I make crazy mistakes late at night only to discover I can fix the problem with a clear head in the morning. In the light of day, it takes minutes rather than hours to make a correction. And never rip out late at night. Step away from the knitting and assess the problem when you are wide awake. It may or may not be time to rip.

• When you get a new pair of circular needles, relax the cord by boiling it. Set a small saucepan of water to a hard boil. Remove the pan from the heat and immerse the cord in the hot water for thirty to sixty seconds. Then while it's cooling, hold it out straight. This will not take all the spring out of the cord, but it will make it more manageable.

• When adding a new thread of color or changing balls at the end of a row, tie a simple overhand knot around the existing yarn to add the new yarn. This will keep things tight and tidy. You can undo the knot when you weave in the ends.

• Bind off loosely. There is a trick to make sure this happens. If you go up a needle size, you are guaranteed to have a loose bind off. The edge will lie flatter when it's loose. I recently worked a lace pattern that instructed me to go up four needle sizes to get the correct effect.

• Exercise your brain and speed up your counting. Knitters are always checking and rechecking the stitch count on the needles. Did I cast on the right number? How many stitches until the pattern change? Try counting by 3s or 4s instead of every single stitch. It goes faster. Every time I count off stitches I hear the *School House Rock* song in my head: 3-6-9, 12-15-18, 21-24-27. Give it a whirl.

• If your current project is not giving you joy, start something new. It's okay to take a break from a difficult or tedious project. Find one that makes your needles hum. Knitting is a gift to bring you joy, not a chore to slog through. It is okay to have more than one project going at a time. I need at least three: one for TV watching that does not require much concentration, a small one that travels well for carpooling and waiting in line, and a big one that is more complicated, just for the thrill of it. And there is always the possibility of finding a terrific new project that has to jump the queue so I can start *right now.*

Starting a Knitting Group

Finding a new knitting friend is the best. And joining a knit circle expands your expertise and gives you a ready audience to applaud when you finish a project. This group of people can help you not only through your latest knitting project but also with life's little knots as well. Playing with yarn draws the group together, but members are often linked together by more than just a fondness for knitting.

Sounds great, right? Where can you find such a happy place? Your local knit shop may already have a knit night or an afternoon circle meeting. But if the "local" shop is miles away, how about starting your own group? Check to see if a group already exists in your area; you may want to join forces. If not, starting your own group is easier than you think.

First decide what kind of group you want. Are you interested in a few friends meeting informally at a coffee shop once a week? Do you want a more formal atmosphere where you can invite guest speakers? Do you picture a group knitting for charity? Or a gathering of knitters working on their latest projects? And how big do you envision your group? Do you want a small group of close friends or a big group of new friends? Thinking this through before you start will help you create the knitting circle you want. And five Ps will get you started: people, publicity, place, plan, and party.

People. Start with a list of interested people: friends, co-workers, family members, and online acquaintances. To grow your group even more, you'll want to publicize. (More on that coming up.) You will need to invite about twice as many knitters as the group size you envision. So if you contact thirty people, expect about a dozen to show up.

Recruiting all skill levels strengthens your group. As you continue to meet, the novices improve and the experienced get a chance to pass along their expertise. Nothing cements skills faster than teaching someone else. Newbies often have such a different perspective, giving a longtime knitter a fresh take on her familiar craft. Depending on the time you meet, you'll be able to include different age levels too. Knitting was once passed along from grandmother to granddaughter. How neat to have a multigenerational group sharing the gift of knitting.

Publicity. Time to get out the word. A personal invitation is always good. "I'm starting a knitting group, and it would be great if you joined us." People are more apt to think seriously about joining when they've been personally invited. And you may find someone to help with the organizing this way. For your group to take hold, you will want to expand your reach from your initial list of friends to include the community. Your group will be stronger and more diverse this way. You'll also get a chance to meet many new knitters and make a wider circle of friends.

The information in your publicity should include the name of your group, the meeting place, the date and time of the first meeting, and contact information, either an email address or phone number. Try these suggestions to get the word out into the community:

- place an ad in a local giveaway paper
- put up flyers at health food stores, the local library, or on other community message boards
- post your notice on Facebook
- send a tweet on Twitter
- put an invitation on Ravelry.com

Many local papers have a calendar section where you can post announcements of your upcoming meeting. Once you establish your group, you can call the local paper and offer to write an article about your group. You can suggest they do a human-interest story on your group, which may also boost membership.

Place. Picking a neutral spot relieves you from having it in your home. My house is not big enough for a large group to sit comfortably and work. Find a place that is free and convenient, such as a meeting room at a local library, community center, rec center, or coffeehouse. Other meeting rooms may be available for a small fee. Try churches, restaurants, and meeting halls for Elks, Kiwanis, and other organizations.

Maybe you can find a meeting room where you work. In fact, think about starting a group at work. Knitting at lunchtime makes a great break in the day.

If you decide to meet at a coffeehouse or restaurant, check with the owner first. Don't assume they will welcome you. Your group may attract business, but you don't want to distract from business either. Be friendly and willing to work with their rules and concerns. It may be as easy as picking a time when the place is not too busy. Your group may decide to charge dues so you can meet in a more private place.

When checking out a spot to meet, look for these things: a location central to most members of the group, a well-lit and smoke-free environment, and flexible seating so you can move the chairs in a circle and have tables to spread out your work.

Plan. Your group will be competing with many other activities in the busy lives of your knitters. Make a good impression at your first meeting. Be organized, relaxed, and welcoming to your guests.

The first meeting will be organizational. Long before you step in the door, get an agenda ready. Write the list on a large sheet of paper that you can post for all to see. Your meeting may look something like this: welcome, introductions, icebreaker, purpose of the group, time for sharing projects, refreshments, future meeting schedule, closing.

Arrive at your meeting half an hour early, allowing plenty of time for setup. You will want to have a welcome table with a sign-in sheet to collect contact information. You will need name tags. Make it easy on your guests to get to know one another. If you had to pay for the meeting place, put out a basket to collect donations to defray the cost. On another table you may want to display knitting samples, books, and magazines. Few knitters can resist perusing such items, and these make good conversation starters.

Give stragglers a few minutes to get settled, but try to start on time. Begin with a pleasant welcome and an introduction of the organizers. Then offer a short explanation as to why you are starting a knitting group. It can be as simple as, "I want to expand my group of knitting friends and become a better knitter."

Try this icebreaker idea that will connect your group, literally. (Arrange your chairs in a circle at setup time.) While holding a ball of yarn in your hand, tell the group your name, how long you've been knitting, and why you came. Then, while holding one end of the yarn, toss the ball to someone across the circle and let that person answer the questions. In the end, the group will be connected. It's a strong visual and fun beginning.

Now take time to explain your vision for the group, and then open the floor for discussion. After some conversation, a purpose should unfold. It might be to learn new techniques and share ideas and a love of knitting. People may also be motivated to use their time and skills to work on charity knitting. Together you are forming the group of which you all want to be a part.

Next, take a break. Most people probably came with a current project they want to show off. Give them a chance to share and talk about what they brought. Have a little show-and-tell.

Refreshments can be a touchy subject with knitters. Many don't want food around their projects. However, few can resist a tempting treat. Your group should discuss how you want to handle refreshments at future meetings. Talk it out and see what options suit your group the best.

Finally, set up future meetings. Someone may suggest changing the time or day of the week, but as the organizer, you get to stand firm on your selection. Try to make the day easy to remember: the first Tuesday of every month or every Friday, for example. If you keep changing the date to accommodate people, you will never settle on a time. Once the next meeting is finalized, you can adjourn. Or you may want to pull out your needles and actually knit if time allows.

Party. This is the easy part: enjoy your group. It will take a little work to keep things going, but attending regularly, keeping the atmosphere positive, and remembering you are there to have fun will keep your group going for years.

To recap, here are the five steps to starting a knitting group:

1. People. Make a list of as many knitters as you can think of.
2. Publicity. Get the word out, advertise your group.
3. Place. Find a central location.
4. Plan. Decide on the format and structure of your meetings.
5. Party. Enjoy your new knitting friends.

Favorites in My Knit Library

I go to bookstores with as much glee as I enter yarn shops. I panic a little if I don't have a good read on my nightstand, just as I panic a little if I have to wait for yarn to arrive in the mail when I order online. My home office is stuffed with books and yarn.

Here are some titles from my knitting library. Some are pattern or technique books I use often; others I reread when I need a little escape. Hopefully you'll find some new inspiration as well as rediscover old friends.

Field Guide to Knitting by Jackie Pawlowski

I'll confess one of the reasons I picked up this book was its size. I love little books. This one fits nicely in my knit bag and is a compact stitch dictionary. I prefer this one for its concise organization and tons of information. Each stitch is beautifully photographed in the middle section of the book, and for each stitch Jackie provides the properties, yarn consumption, and suggested uses. So you will know if a stitch is reversible, rolls at the edges, or has some other noteworthy quality. The yarn consumption section is invaluable when trying to plan a project. Even if you are just testing out a new stitch for a scarf, you'll want to know if it will eat through the yarn or be more economical. The only drawback of the book is that the stitch photos are not next to their patterns, so you have to do some flipping between pages, but otherwise this is a great book.

Knitting Rules! by Stephanie Pearl-McPhee

I am not alone in my enthusiasm for just about anything Stephanie writes. And she has many titles to choose from. *At Wit's End* is another favorite. But *Knitting Rules!* holds a special place in my heart: I got my son to read it. When my son was ten, we were reading books together one evening.

His was *The Botany of Desire*, and I was reading *Knitting Rules!* We took turns sharing facts with each other. He fed me interesting food facts, and I giggled over knit-bits I had to share. Finally, he asked me if we could trade books. Sure. *This won't last long.* But soon he was reading aloud a paragraph here and there. I love it that he laughed in all the right places.

This book is funny, yes, but it also gives clear information on knitting from cast on to bind off. Swatching, gauge, tools—you name it—are all explained. There are many how-to knitting books but few with such humor.

The Secret Language of Knitters by Mary Beth Temple

This is another pocket-sized book filled with knitting knowledge, and it's laugh out loud funny. You will learn what in the world "LYS," "UFO," and "WIP" stand for, and you'll also find there are others who make their families wait for "the end of the row." Mary Beth demystifies yarn weights and their names. She takes on the quirks of yarn shopping and all kinds of jargon. Even seasoned knitters will find new terms to expand their knitting expertise.

Knitting for Peace: Making the World a Better Place One Stitch at a Time by Betty Christiansen

I'm a sucker for good design, and this is a beautiful book from cover to cover. The photos and the layout are lovely. Betty not only highlights dozens of charities that need knitters but also tells the stories behind the charities. Many started with small ideas from sympathetic knitters. One of those stories may excite you to join a new cause. Betty includes the contact information for all the charities as well as patterns to get you started. It is heartwarming to know there are so many ways knitters are sharing their craft and making a difference.

Beyond Stitch and Bitch: Reflections on Knitting and Life by Afi-Odelia Scruggs

I am drawn to the knit section of every bookstore I visit. I never know what treasure I may find. Afi-Odelia's little book was tucked in an independent bookstore. Her thoughts on knitting made me nod in agreement. But she went further and showed me the knitting perspective of an African-American woman knitting in the South. Her experience is very different from mine. I was delighted to see how knitting unites us.

Knitting America: A Glorious Heritage from Warm Socks to High Art by Susan M. Strawn

Diving into the history of knitting is fascinating to me. This big coffee-table book is loaded with pictures and an in-depth look at the craft and art of knitting. Susan puts a face on every decade, taking us through each era and showcasing how knitting is in the very fabric of our country. I learned many interesting tidbits.

In my library, technique books and essay collections share shelf space with the knitting-themed fiction I enjoy. Knitting circles lend themselves to great stories. With a ready-made cast of characters around the circle, it's easy for the author to dive into their lives and weave them together. Several goodies fall into this category.

The Shop on Blossom Street by Debbie Macomber

This book begins a delightful series of five. After writing *The Shop on Blossom Street*, Debbie received so many letters from readers asking what happened next to the ladies at the knit shop that the stand-alone book became a terrific series. We meet all kinds of characters, from business owners on Blossom Street to the people taking knitting classes at the shop, aptly named A Good Yarn. As you walk into the shop for the first time, it's great to know you don't have to leave for five books!

Friday Night Knitting Club by Kate Jacobs

Kate's knitters are young, old, single, married, widowed, and divorced. There's sure to be a character with whom you can identify. The story focuses on the Walker and Daughter Shop in New York but takes you as far as Scotland and back again. Good thing this book is part of a series. You won't want to leave after one installment.

Chicks with Sticks by Elizabeth Lenhard

This is yet another book in a series. You can see I like to stay and knit with characters for a while. These chicks are a little different; they're high schoolers. Before you skip by thinking these young adult novels aren't for you, pause a moment. These stories are well written, it's fun to remember high school, and the overlay of knitting is cool. It's the story of four friends woven together by knitting. They are not all that enthusiastic about the craft in the beginning. It's delightful to see how knitting takes root in their lives.

Beach Street Knitting Society and Yarn Club by Gil McNeil

I love the BBC and all things British. This story begins in London, and then we are carried into a small town in the English countryside where our heroine, recently widowed, and her two young sons have inherited a knitting shop. This is a satisfying read with a wide range of characters. Gil has also written a sequel called *Needles and Pearls*.

The Sweetgum Knit Lit Society: A Novel by Beth Pattillo

The knit circle in Sweetgum is a literary group as well as a knitting group. The town librarian runs the group. Each month they read a book and complete a related knit project. Of course, in the time between meetings we learn what's going on in their lives, which are skillfully stitched together. Happily, there is a sequel: *The Sweetgum Ladies Knit for Love*.

The Knitting Circle by Ann Hood

After reading the teaser on the dust jacket, I wasn't sure I would continue. The main character loses her child. But of course knitting helps save her. Each knitter in the circle tells a story of woe, and the stories gently help the heroine in the healing process from her loss. This circle of characters reminded me that we all have burdens to carry and that knitting makes them a little more bearable.

Websites to Enjoy, or Knitting in Cyberspace

Knitting has so many angles. There are techniques to master. Patterns to hunt for. Yarn to drool over. Friends to chat with. All these things can happen in cyberspace.

One of the best things about the internet is finding knitting help whenever you need it. You may have laughed when you read about Mike learning to make buttonholes off a website in Portuguese. But I was inspired. Whenever my knitting is in a tangle, I can find help with the click of a button. *Which way does a yarnover go? How do you make a three-stitch buttonhole? Show me an ssk (slip slip knit).* Type your question into YouTube and you will find many knitters waiting to help you, and in English too!

Surfing the web can use up a lot of valuable knitting time. I don't venture out too often. But these are a few of the websites I enjoy.

Ravelry.com

This is an online knitting community. It is a site you join for free. Ravelry offers a place to manage your knit life as well as meet other knitters and see what they are up to. You can enter your entire stash to keep track of yarn you have. There is place to keep track of your needle collection too. You can call it up on your smart phone while you are out shopping (or ask the store if you can use their internet connection) and check on your needs before you purchase duplicate twenty-four-inch size 8 circulars. (Though really you can never have too many size 8s.)

This is just the beginning with Ravelry, though. Its claim to fame and the thing I use the website for the most is its display of creations by talented knitters. If you want to see what a pattern looks like made up, you can see hundreds of examples. You can find the modifications people have used to make a pattern work or take it to the next level. Ravelry also has hundreds of group discussion boards. You can find a connection, no matter how specific. It is *the* website to connect to the knitting community. You can find me on the site as LisaWriter.

Patternfish.com

Browsing patterns is a pastime of mine. I am often on the lookout for my next great sweater project. This site offers a wide variety of patterns for sale. The designers will get the fruits of their labors. Each pattern is marked for your personal use once you download it.

Twistcollective.com

I fell in love with a Kate Gilbert sweater design. I checked out her site and then followed her to twistcollective.com. Kate is one of the creative forces behind this online knit magazine. The patterns are great, and it's a well-organized site. It's fun to see what the twist gang is up to each season. There always seems to be something I want to add to my project queue.

Etsy.com

This site is a collection of artist shops offering all kinds of unique art items to purchase, from origami boxes to beaded earrings to woven scarves to yarn. I love to see what spinners are up to and what they have to offer. This is a fun site to browse for yarn and other goodies.

Knitting wisdom is fun to share whether you get it from a good book, a favorite website, or a knitting buddy in a new knit circle. I hope you've found some things in this chapter that you will use to help your knitting flow. We've almost come to the end of our project. It's time to bind off and weave in the loose ends.

10

Bind Off

Loose Ends

Bind off: to finish with a stitch or row of stitches and take the project off the needles completely.

Every pattern ends with finishing instructions—all those little details to make your knitting complete. Add the buttons to the cardigan. Weave in the ends so they don't unravel. We've come to the end of this pattern, the last chapter. It's time for us to weave in the loose ends.

It has been fun to introduce you to the many knitters in this book. Sometimes, though, there is more to the story.

Most of the stories in this book are a snapshot of a knitter's adventure. Many knit as a lifestyle. I was able to show you only a brief picture of one adventure. The knitters shared other fascinating details with me, and I'd love to weave in a few more details. Knitting is not a single act but an activity that's part of a bigger lifetime of joy and service. So here are some of the loose ends.

When Staff Sergeant John Sorich IV came home from Iraq, one of his stops was Needlework Unlimited in Minneapolis. He wanted to share his knitting with the women there and thank them for keeping him supplied with yarn while he was deployed. The women were touched and honored. John's homecoming was written up in the *Star Tribune* of Minneapolis/St. Paul. From that interview, the Minnesota Knitting Guild heard about John, and he was asked to share his story for the June 2010 meeting. He talked for an hour about his knitting adventures. The group was so fascinated that they kept him for a half hour of questions. John is still a knitter. For John, knitting is not just a stress release; it's a pleasure.

After taking down the Christmas tree decorated with knitted baby things, Ann Ellington Wagner delivered them to the local hospital. The director of the neonatal unit suggested she try teaching some of the moms there to knit. Depression strikes often. Anything that will provide a diversion for the parents whose baby must stay for months is good. Ann found a new phase of her knitting adventure. She gathered some simple patterns along with yarn and needles. Chat and Knit (or crochet) isn't a full-blown program yet, but it's a lovely continuation of what knitting can do. Worried parents have a chance to talk about their fears and anxieties while making something with love for their little ones.

Sue Thompson does so much charity work that it's hard to keep up with her. When she was telling me about her Head Huggers group, she also shared her prison knitting. Like Judy Ditmore, Sue discovered that working in the prison system can be frustrating, with all its rules, but also very rewarding. It is one of Sue's favorite ministries.

Audrey Fisher has knit friends in knit shops across the country. She recently got the chance to make another group of friends. While working in Atlanta, she was asked by a church group to help them learn to knit. This group of women crochets blankets for nursing home residents. Some in their group wanted to start knitting them as well. Audrey was up for teaching them. "You know, these women have been making blankets for nursing home residents for years. Each season they send out a scout, one of the women in the group who volunteers to find a new place that needs blankets. They find out the number of residents. Then they spend the next year making a blanket for every bed in the residence, sometimes as many as two hundred. I had to be a part of that."

The fifty scarves our church group made for the homeless last year was just that, a project for last year. But the need arises annually, and so we are gearing up to make scarves again. The people in our congregation who work in the soup kitchen are ready to help distribute them. For me, this means

I'll knit in church. What better advertisement for our cause than to knit scarves at church? It gets others interested in joining us. Maybe we'll be able to provide even more than seventy-six this year.

I hope you have fallen in love with knitting all over again. I also hope you continue to use this book as a resource. When you want to cast on a new project, maybe you'll go looking for a charity to support from chapter 6. When you want some encouragement with your knitting, you can look in chapter 2. When you want to smile over some crazy things knitters do, you can look again at stories about Knitting Olympics or yarnbombing. Or when you just want to sit with a new knit friend, you can pull out a book recommendation from chapter 9.

You've met some interesting knitters in these pages. Lloyd Harvey still knitting daily at age 106. Ann Gussiff knitting a piece of family history. Marlene Reilly and her niece celebrating knitting with an annual vacation. We are all part of the same circle; we are knit together with our love of the craft. We're knitters. We can start up a friendship just by asking, "What are you working on?" May the new friends you've met here call to mind other friends you want to sit and knit with in person, sharing life. And if you are still searching for local knitters, try starting a group of your own. You will be delighted you did.

Rejoice in the craft of knitting. It is a gift you've been given. You benefit from it physically with a calm heart and a peaceful mind. You benefit from it emotionally and spiritually with the warm feelings of help and purpose. And you have a finished product to share with someone. New projects pop up, new ways to share your gift come to mind. I hope you will continue to find joy with yarn and sticks, whether you give away every item you make or you knit sweaters for family and friends and pray for them as you knit. Find ways to keep the love on your needles.

Writing about knitting delights me. Listening to all the wonderful things knitters have to say about their craft inspires me. But writing this book was one of the hardest things I've ever done. I had little time to actually knit! I snuck in a few projects—a pair of socks, a quick hat, a short scarf—but nothing big. Now the stories are told, and I can cast on something time consuming. I found a tunic-length, fair-isle sweater I am excited to start as soon as I can. And I'll breathe in the benefits and think of all my new knitting readers as I work.

We've finished the last stitch, anchored the last thread. Now it's time for you to select a new project. Take your eager hands and knit something with love.

Happy knitting,

Appendix

Websites

www.massgeneral.org/bhi/
  Benson-Henry Institute for Mind Body Medicine
www.stitchlinks.com
  connecting people using knitting to manage health issues
www.iknitlinks.org
  connecting the knit community online
www.knitforkids.org
  Guideposts knitting project
www.craftyarncouncil.com/warmup.html
  Warm Up America!
www.headhuggers.org
  chemo caps
www.miracleshappen.us
  charity for babies in need and their moms
www.operationtoastytoes.org
  slippers for the military

www.piedmontyarn.com
Oakland, California, yarn shop making a community difference
www.saigonchildren.com
Saigon Children's Charities
www.wateraid.org
International WaterAid
www.thestitchinden.com
Estes Park, Colorado, yarn shop sponsoring Happy Stitches baskets
www.lifewind.org
holistic ministry meeting physical and spiritual needs
www.yarnharlot.ca/blog/
Stephanie Pearl-McPhee's blog
www.ravelry.com
online knitting community
www.patternfish.com
hundreds of patterns for sale
www.twistcollective.com
online knit magazine
www.etsy.com
all kinds of crafts for sale: yarn to finished products

Notes

Chapter 4 Continue in Established Pattern

1. Susan M. Strawn, *Knitting America: A Glorious Heritage from Warm Socks to High Art* (St. Paul, MN: Voyageur Press, 2007), 16, 44, 46.

2. Betty Christiansen, *Knitting for Peace* (St. Paul, MN: Stewart, Tabori & Chang, 2006), 13.

3. Strawn, *Knitting America*, 25.

4. Ibid., 44, 46.

5. Ibid., 45–46.

6. Anne L. Macdonald, *No Idle Hands: The Social History of American Knitting* (New York: Ballantine Books, 1988), 112.

7. Strawn, *Knitting America*, 140.

8. "How to Knit," *Life*, November 24, 1941, 111.

9. Strawn, *Knitting America*, 103.

Chapter 5 At the Same Time

1. See www.massgeneral.org/bhi.

2. www.massgeneral.org/bhi/basics/eliciting_rr.aspx.

MEET
Lisa Bogart at
www.lisabogart.com

- Read her weekly thoughts
- Enter special drawings and contests
- Discover monthly surprises
- And more!

Join Ravelry.com today
and find Lisa at **r** LisaWriter.
Like Lisa at **f** LisaBogartAuthor.